OUR FINEST HOUR

The Triumphant Spirit of the World War II Generation

Lt. Paul Fisher Jr., of Bronxville, N.Y., is grateful to his battle-damaged P-38: It carried him to Berlin—and back to his base in England.

Editor
Killian Jordan

Picture Editor
Barbara Baker Burrows

Art Director
Ian Denning

Time Inc.
HOME ENTERTAINMENT

**Five thousand
soldiers at Fort Bragg,
N.C., April 6, 1942**

OUR FINEST HOUR

**The Triumphant Spirit
of the World War II
Generation**

"Future generations may dismiss the
Second World War as 'just another
war.' Those who experienced it know that it
was a war justified in its aims and successful in
accomplishing them. Despite all the killing
and destruction that accompanied it,
the Second World War was a good war. "
—A.J.P. Taylor, *The Second World War*

IN THE MIDDLE OF THE COUNTRY, IN THE MIDDLE OF THE CENTURY

By Bob Greene

In the house where I grew up, there was a portrait hanging on the wall of the first floor, not far from the kitchen.

It was not a famous painting, not the work of a well-known artist. In fact, even though, in my mind's eye, it is the most memorable portrait I have ever encountered, I still have no idea of precisely who held the brush and applied the oil to the canvas.

I do know that the portrait was done in Italy, during World War II, and that the artist was an Army buddy of my father's. Apparently this man enjoyed painting portraits for his fellow soldiers in the 91st Infantry Division, and he did them during down moments in the long months the 91st spent in North Africa and Italy in 1944 and 1945. The artist's subject—the man whose face looks off the canvas—was my dad.

He virtually never spoke about the painting; it was on the wall of our house all during my childhood, and later, when he and my mother moved to another house, they took it with them. Today the portrait hangs on a wall in the house where my mother lives by herself, now that he is dead.

The years of the war were—I now know—the most important and affecting of his life, the years of which he was the very proudest. If you were to have asked him—which I don't think we ever did—what was the best accomplishment of his lifetime, I am quite certain he would have said, without hesitation: serving in the United States Army in the greatest conflict in the history of man.

Not that he was a hero, or a renowned soldier; he was neither. He was there. That was enough—he, like all those American soldiers and sailors and airmen of the war years, was there. He knew he did not face the daily peril that the frontline guys, the dogfaces, did, and he never pretended that it was otherwise. But he was there—in Africa, in Italy, on the long march through the Apennine mountains and then, when the victory in Europe was won, back through Bologna and Florence and Naples—and it was the period of his manhood that mattered most. It was—unsentimentally—the time of his life.

Perhaps, when he was alone with our mother, he spoke in detail of those days and nights, but to us children he talked of the war only in the most general of ways. It was almost as if he thought he would bore us if he told us war stories; it was almost as though he didn't want us to think him tedious.

Yet there was the portrait in our house—on a quiet street in the middle of Ohio in the middle of the country in the middle of the century. There were no mementos of the war in our home—when I was in the first and second and third grade, World War II had been over for less than 10 years, but there were no souvenirs, no displays. Save for the portrait his fellow soldier had painted.

All of them—all of those young men whose lives had been difficult enough during the years of the Depression, and then all of a sudden their worlds were jarred once more, this time by events in countries that, as Depression boys, they never even dared to dream of visiting. And then they were there. They were on the ground in those distant nations that had been colors on a classroom globe to them. No one promised them they would ever get to come back home.

And—most remarkable of all—they seldom spoke about it. Those who did make it home—those who survived the fighting—went about their lives, and started families, and reported to work in a different America, an America of the postvictory years in which the former soldiers were expected to wear different uniforms, obey different rules. They became the men in the gray flannel suits—or the factory coveralls, or the service-station caps and slacks—and it was almost as if they thought they were supposed to forget about the war, except for inside their own hearts. It was almost as if—no one told them this, they must have decided it on their own—they felt they were obliged to keep it to themselves.

My father, before he died, recorded a tape about his

From Camp Shelby (above), the author's father went to Officer Candidate School, then on to Oregon and the 91st Infantry Division.

life, a gift to my sister and brother and me. It wasn't a professional production; over the course of weeks or months, he spoke the words into a handheld tape recorder. There were stories of his childhood, and of his young adulthood, and there were stories of him as a married man and a father and, eventually, a grandfather.

But the guts of his life story—the solid center—was the narrative of his years at war. Most of it, the first time I heard the tape, was brand new to me; these were the most elemental stories of his time on earth, but I didn't know them.

One passage in particular—after he had been drafted into the Army and sent to Camp Shelby in Hattiesburg, Mississippi, for basic training—stops me every time I listen to it. I have to remind myself that these young men, most of them, had never been soldiers before; these young men had had very little time to process what had just happened to them. One day they were walking the streets of their hometowns in that pre-interstate-highway America that was so much more local than the America in which we live today; the next day they were being told that they were soldiers in training to win what would turn out to be the most massive global war in history.

Here is the passage—my father describing some of those first days of basic training, into which he had entered scared and disoriented and so far away from everyone and everything with which he was familiar:

After we got down to Camp Shelby, it was an entirely new world. The camp had recently been gouged out of cornfields and cotton fields, and consisted of miles and miles of perimeter tents with wood-and-coal-burning stoves in them. And that was our introduction to Army life. The first thing we noted was a cloud of black smoke over the whole area as far as you could see, a result of the soft coal that was being burnt in those stoves. It was the middle of winter, and while the camp was in Mississippi it was still a very cold place, and the stoves were badly needed. We lined up and were assigned certain companies . . .

In the meantime, a strange phenomenon occurred. As you know, the favorite thing for a soldier to do is gripe, and believe me, this division made up of fifteen thousand recent civilians and a handful of regular Army officers and enlisted men did very little else but gripe. The weather was terrible, the jobs onerous, the drills and hikes very bone-wearying, and in all it was a hell of a way to live.

But the phenomenon I mentioned to you was just this—strangely enough, I started to like it. I don't know why, but it just seemed to me that I was free.

Although I had to obey orders and do everything a soldier must do, it was kind of a newfound freedom. Everyone was alike, nobody was given any privileges other than what they deserved or earned, and I was not fettered by a [civilian] job that I did not like. So going into the Army, believe it or not, was kind of a relief for me . . .

So unexpected—the fine gradations of a man's life, the never-anticipated changes he may encounter, changes that transform him from the person he was before into the person he will be forever after. Showing up for Army training and finding it liberating, finding it freeing . . . so unexpected for him as it happened, so unexpected for his son to learn, all the years later.

They are leaving us every day now, the men and women of these war years; soon we, their children, will be all alone in the world they saved for us. Each of those men, each of those women, had his or her own stories; most of the time, or so it seems, the stories went untold.

He never said—not to my face—just how essential those years in uniform were to the man he became. But he didn't really have to say it. None of them did.

The portrait hung on the wall of a peaceful house in a peaceful town, and of all the times he must have walked past that portrait—on his way to the dinner table, on his way to work, on his way to bed—I don't recall even one occasion when he stopped to stand before it and look into the eyes of the young man he used to be.

Columnist Bob Greene is the author of Duty: A Father, His Son, and the Man Who Won the War.

> " If you were to have asked him—which I don't think we ever did—what was the best accomplishment of his lifetime, I am quite certain he would have said, without hesitation: serving in the United States Army in the greatest conflict in the history of man. "

THE BEGINNING

The Japanese attack on Pearl Harbor (here, the USS *West Virginia* and USS *Tennessee* in flames) precipitates a speech to Congress and the American people by President Roosevelt. Opposite: his revisions on the first draft.

DRAFT No. 1   December 7, 1941.

PROPOSED MESSAGE TO THE CONGRESS

Yesterday, December 7, 1941, a date which will live in ~~world history~~ infamy

the United States of America was ~~simultaneously~~ suddenly and deliberately attacked

by naval and air forces of the Empire of Japan.

The United States was at the moment at peace with that nation and was
~~continuing the~~ still in conversation with its Government and its Emperor looking

toward the maintenance of peace in the Pacific. Indeed, one hour after

Japanese air squadrons had commenced bombing in ~~Hawaii and the Philippines~~ Oahu

the Japanese Ambassador to the United States and his colleague delivered

to the Secretary of State a formal reply to a ~~former~~ recent American message ~~from the~~

~~Secretary.~~ While This reply ~~contained a statement~~ stated that diplomatic negotiations

~~must be considered at an end,~~ it contained no threat ~~and no~~ or hint of ~~an~~ war or

armed attack.

It will be recorded that the distance of

Hawaii from Japan make it obvious that the attack was deliberately

planned many days ago or even weeks. During the intervening time the Japanese Govern-

ment has deliberately sought to deceive the United States by false

statements and expressions of hope for continued peace.

VICTOR BARRON

Lt. Stanley A. Jones, in charge of Navy recruiting for the Georgia-Florida district, swears in a group of volunteers in a Macon, Ga., courtroom.

> "October 3, 1942: I enlisted in the U.S. Navy today. It looks like the Navy got the makings of a very poor sailor when they got me. I still get carsick and cannot ride on a swing for any length of time.
>
> I took my physical examination at the Post Office Building in Boston, Mass., a distance of about ten miles from Waltham, Mass. . . . On the way home I relaxed in the old trolley car and felt like the Fleet Admiral himself."
>
> —James J. Fahey, *Pacific War Diary 1942–1945*

Man the GUNS
Join the **NAVY**

LIBRARY OF CONGRESS

Number of men who entered military service
through the Selective Service System:

Year	Number
1940	18,633
1941	923,842
1942	3,033,361
1943	3,323,970
1944	1,591,942
1945	945,862
1946	183,383

Opposite: A draft service worker. Above: New recruits receive simultaneous smallpox and typhoid injections at Fort Dix, N.J.

" On December 22, twins Harold and Harry Martinson of Roland, Iowa (pop. 900), became 17, minimum naval enlistment age, and 12 days later, with right hands upraised, they swore "true faith and allegiance" to the U.S.A. Outside, the family, their objections swept aside by Pearl Harbor, waited quietly. They had risen at dawn to drive the boys into town through blizzard-drifted roads. On their last night at home, their pastor stopped by to give each boy a copy of the Lutheran Servicemen's Prayer Book to carry with him. "

—LIFE, February 2, 1942

Before they can pack up (above), the boys have to be fingerprinted (right). In uniform at last (opposite), the twins stand beside their newly issued equipment. Their only previous nautical experience has been in a rowboat, but now they will begin deepwater training.

WALLACE KIRKLAND (3)

Recruits on their way to training camp, 1941

VICTOR BARRON

ALFRED EISENSTAEDT

" Each goodbye is a drama complete in itself. Sometimes the girl stands with arms around the boy's waist, hands tightly clasped behind. Another fits her head into the curve of his cheek while tears fall onto his coat. Now and then the boy will take her face between his hands and speak reassuringly. Or if the wait is long they may just stand quietly, not saying anything. The common denominator of all these goodbyes is sadness and tenderness, and complete oblivion for the moment to anything but their own individual heartaches. "

—LIFE, February 14, 1944

" The infantry finally accepted me. I was not overjoyed. The infantry was too commonplace for my ambition. The months would teach me the spirit of this unglamorous, greathearted fighting machine. But at that time I had other plans.

Thus, with a pocket full of holes, a head full of dreams, and an ignorance beyond my years, I boarded a bus for the induction center. Previously I had never been over a hundred miles from home. "

—Audie Murphy, *To Hell and Back*

" I was a pre-med student at Johns Hopkins in civilian life. Now, I do know a little something about anatomy, and I say it's scientifically impossible for the human body to stand up to the training we received. An absolute impossibility. Muscles and tendons and bone structure—it was not designed to withstand that battering. Don't ask me how it happens that we did stand up to it. I don't know. It has no scientific explanation. "

—Serviceman, *The True Glory* (War Department film)

Marines (left) at Montford Point, N.C., run an obstacle course; U.S. Army Rangers (above) in Scotland throw logs from shoulder to shoulder.

MARIE HANSEN

> " The worst example of [the Army Ordnance Department's] doodling in the peacetime years is the U.S. soldier's steel helmet. Knowing full well that the helmet of World War I exposed the wearer's neck to shell fragments and was also uncomfortable, Ordnance delayed adoption of a better helmet. Today, 20 years later, with a crackerjack design in its pocket, Ordnance is delayed in getting production because it can't get enough manganese steel to make it. "
>
> —*Time*, October 27, 1941

CORBIS/UPI/BETTMANN

Army Day parade down New York City's Fifth Avenue, April 1942

Waacs (soon to be Wacs when the word Auxiliary is dropped) practice close-order drill across the parade ground at Fort Des Moines.

HOME FRONT

Rosie the Riveter

While other girls attend their fav'rite cocktail bar
Sipping dry martinis, munching caviar,
There's a girl who's really putting them to shame.
Rosie is her name.
All the day long whether rain or shine,
She's a part of the assembly line.
She's making history working for victory,
Rosie the riveter.
Keeps a sharp lookout for sabotage
Sitting up there on the fuselage.
That little frail can do more than a male can do,
Rosie the riveter.
Rosie's got a boyfriend, Charlie.
Charlie, he's a Marine
Rosie, is protecting Charlie
Working overtime on the riveting machine.
When they gave her a production "E"
She was as proud as a girl could be.
There's something true about,
Red, white and blue about
Rosie the riveter.

—Lyric and music by Redd Evans
and John Jacob Loeb

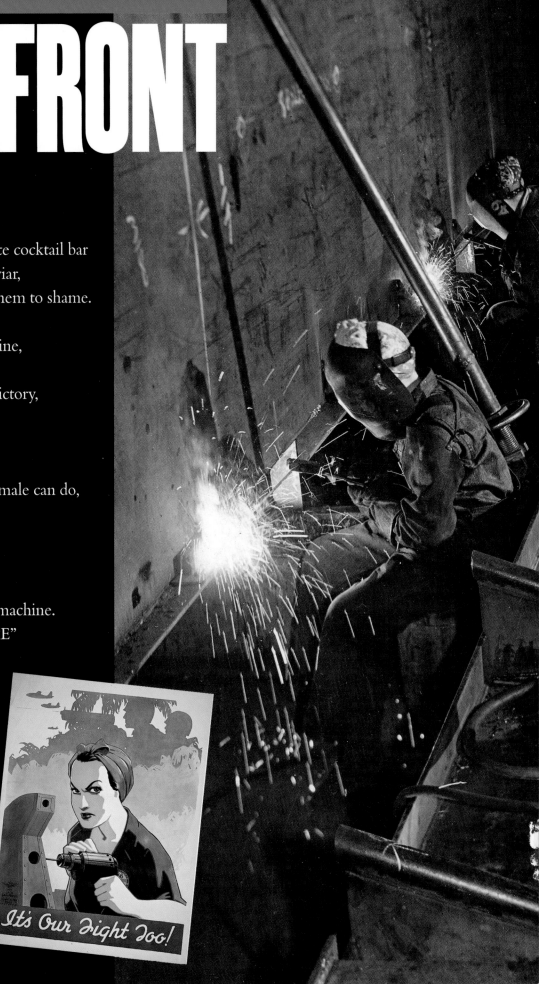

It's Our Fight Too!

Women work eight hours a day, six days a week. Minimum pay is 78 cents per hour; a weekly wage is at least $40.56.

CULVER PICTURES

MARGARET BOURKE-WHITE

In 1941 only 1 percent of aviation employees were women; this year they will make up some 65 percent of the total. Of the 16 million women now employed in the U.S., over a quarter are in war industries. But until recently only a small percentage has been used to replace men in heavy industry. Although the concept of the weaker sex sweating near blast furnaces is accepted in England and Russia, it has always been foreign to American tradition. Only the rising need for labor has forced this revolutionary adjustment.

—LIFE, August 9, 1943

CAROL EYERMAN

Penitentiary and reformatory workers build Army patrol boats (above) and bomb fins (below), and stitch flags (right). Inmates operate farms, donate blood and have purchased $7,825 in war bonds from prison earnings.

K. CHESTER

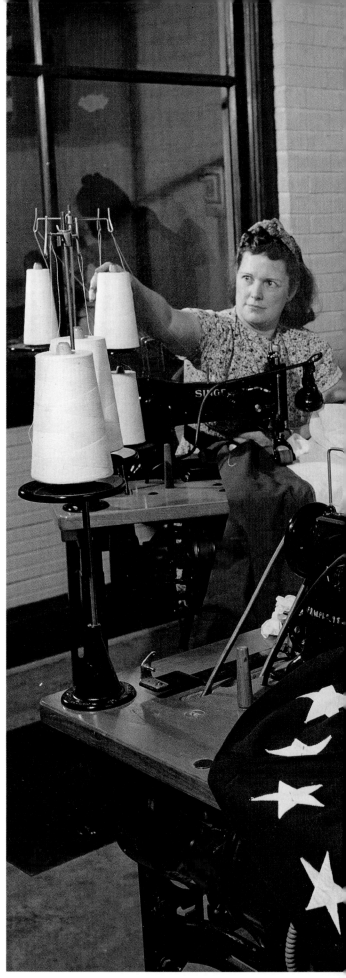

> U.S. prisons contain 150,000 men capable of producing more than $100 million worth of war goods this year. Said a prisoner at San Quentin, 'We know what freedom means.'
> —LIFE, December 7, 1942

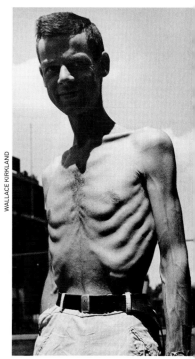

After five months in a volunteer starvation study, Samuel Legg has lost 35 pounds.

WALLACE KIRKLAND

" In a 40-room laboratory housed in the football stadium at the University of Minnesota, 34 young men are being systematically starved. They are conscientious objectors from all over the U.S. who volunteered as 'guinea pigs' in a scientific study of starvation. Its immediate object is to find out the best way to rehabilitate the hunger-wasted millions of Europe.

Mentally the men feel a general lethargy, having little interest in conversation or sex. They complain of feeling 'old.' They report an inability to keep warm, average body temperature being 95.8°F.

The single consuming thought uppermost in their minds, day and night, is food. They love to plan meals, spend hours with lavishly illustrated cookbooks and have guilty nightmares in which they dream of feasting on huge meals.

Now in the diet's sixth and last month, the volunteers will be given a three-month rehabilitation diet. Many of them wish to go to stricken areas to add their firsthand knowledge of the problem. "

—LIFE, July 30, 1945

ALBERT FENN

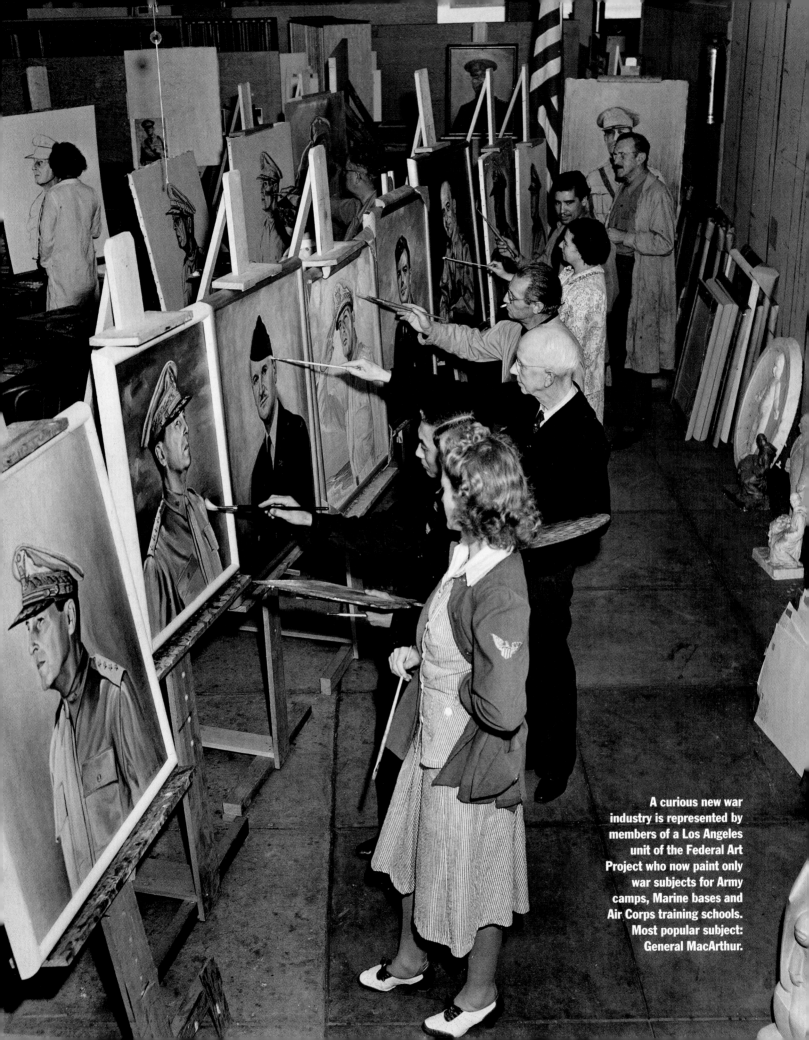

A curious new war industry is represented by members of a Los Angeles unit of the Federal Art Project who now paint only war subjects for Army camps, Marine bases and Air Corps training schools. Most popular subject: General MacArthur.

> There was a joke that made the rounds of wartime Washington. A man crossing the Fourteenth Street bridge looked down into the Potomac and saw another man drowning. 'What's your name and address?' he shouted to him and then ran off to see the drowning man's landlord. He asked to rent the now-vacant room and was told it was already taken. 'But I just left him drowning in the river,' he protested. 'That's right,' the landlord replied, 'but the man who pushed him in got here first.'
>
> —David Brinkley, *Washington Goes to War*

Owing to the heavy influx of defense workers, life in the nation's capital is so cramped that employees like these must sleep in shifts. One of the girls works nights, so only three need sleep at one time.

"We'll have lots to eat this winter, won't we Mother?"

**Grow your own
Can your own**

GRANGER COLLECTION

Estimates are that even a city garden will produce at least $10 worth of vegetables.

> The Agriculture Department hopes that, because of Victory gardens (as many as 18 million of them), food rationing will have much less sting this summer. The department emphasizes that gardening is work as well as fun, requires sound planning as well as patriotism.
>
> For all the precautions, though, 1943's Victory gardens will still produce many a laugh for professional farmers. One Dallas newsman bought a pound of turnip seed (enough for an acre) for his modest back yard. Seed companies have received dozens of inquiries for coffee seed, even got one request for succotash seed.
>
> —*Time,* February 8, 1943

❝ Uncle Sam last week assumed the role of fashion designer. Sweeping restrictions aim to save 15 percent of the yardage now used in women's and girls' apparel through such measures as restricting hems and belts to two inches, eliminating cuffs on sleeves. Exempt categories include bridal gowns, maternity dresses, vestments for religious orders. **❞**

—LIFE, April 20, 1942

NINA LEEN (2)

BLACK STAR

CORBIS/UPI/BETTMANN

“ A granite precedent was shattered, a male stronghold crumbled, and stock trading was enlivened last week when a woman went to work on the floor of the New York Stock Exchange for the first time in 150 years. She was good-looking, young (18), auburn-haired, and plainly garbed. Nevertheless, there was excitement, and will be more. ”

—*Time*, May 10, 1943

Some 3,600 male workers from the Stock Exchange and its member firms are in the armed forces. Women (in NYSE uniforms) have begun replacing them.

SAM SHERE

Girls in New Jersey (left) mount a record-setting scrap paper drive, while children of the Grand Street Settlement (opposite) on Manhattan's Lower East Side conduct a lively aluminum salvage campaign.

" Householders find it hard to refuse cooperation when these children extract promises for salvage paper. The Girl Scouts and Brownies helped the town of Livingston, N.J., run up a record collection of 100 pounds per person. In 13 collections during the past year, Livingston's 6,500 people have harvested more than 350 tons of waste paper. "

—LIFE, June 5, 1944

AP

Mrs. Bowen hasn't been any too well during the past few years and has been unable to get up into her attic and give it a really thorough cleaning out.

> Paper mills, steel mills, rubber plants, all kinds of factories will languish unless their dwindling supplies of scrap and waste materials are increased. Most of the laggard U.S. doesn't understand or care.
>
> Binghamton, N.Y., however, is a shining example: Its salvage is well organized; it makes regular collections; householders get rid of junk quickly. Special trips are made for big cleanups, like the memorable clearing of Jenny Bowen's attic.

—LIFE, March 2, 1942

A special crew of salvage men took what Mrs. Bowen didn't want and left a few things she couldn't bear to part with.

The end result is shown with Mrs. Bowen: 150 pounds of scrap iron, 100 pounds of rags, 250 pounds of paper.

WILLIAM VANDIVERT (3)

Schumak made no effort to resist but asserted that he had wanted the scrap pile as an investment for his old age.

In Valparaiso, Ind., March 13, soldiers and agents of the War Production Board invaded the junk yard of Frank Schumak and carried away 200,000 pounds of scrap metal that he had refused to sell at the Government's price of $18.75 a ton. Schumak had allegedly jeered, 'If the Government wants it, they'd better send along the Army.' The War Production Board took him at his word.

—LIFE, March 30, 1942

When they had gone, he ripped off his cap and gloves, hurled them to the ground and stamped on them hard.

HERBERT MCLAUGHLIN/MERCURY PICTURES (2)

Hollywood supports the war effort with films like
This Is the Army and *Casablanca* (above), in which
Humphrey Bogart tells Ingrid Bergman, as war rages
in Europe, that their romantic problems "don't
amount to a hill of beans in this crazy world."

" At every opportunity, naturally and inconspicuously,
show people making small sacrifices for victory—
making them voluntarily, cheerfully and because of the
people's own sense of responsibility, not because of any
laws. For example, show people bringing their own sugar
when invited out to dinner, carrying their own parcels
when shopping, travelling on planes or trains with light
luggage, uncomplainingly giving up seats for servicemen
or others travelling on war priorities; show persons
accepting dimout restrictions, tire and gas rationing
cheerfully, show well-dressed persons, obviously car
owners, riding in crowded buses and streetcars. "

—Instructions to the movie industry, from the Bureau
of Motion Pictures in the Office of War Information

Fans have been surprised by the abilities of wartime subs like major leaguer Pete Gray (left) and girls' baseball and softball teams. Sliding home, Freda Savona (right) of the New Orleans Jax Brewers bats over .400 and is considered best in her sport.

UPI/CORBIS-BETTMANN

FPG

> At a time when disabled veterans were returning from the fighting front in increasing numbers, [Pete Gray of the St. Louis Browns] became a symbol of how to overcome a handicap courageously. He was the most talked-about rookie of the year and a drawing card at the box office . . . He was an excellent outfielder, trapping the ball in his glove, then in a quick motion throwing the ball in the air, cramming his glove under the stump of his right arm and quickly plucking the ball and throwing it with his now bare hand. Gray lasted one season in the majors. He played in 77 games and batted .218, with 51 hits—all but eight of which were singles.

—Richard Lingeman, *Don't You Know There's a War On?*

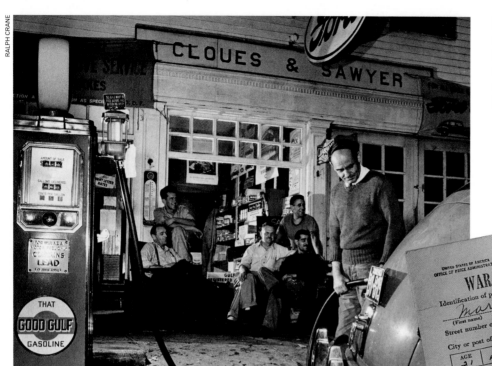

RALPH CRANE

KARI HAAVISTO

Rationing of fuel and food does not seem unreasonable to Alfred Cloues, co-owner of this Warner, N.H., gas station. His son Eddie was killed at Pearl Harbor.

> The man thanked Mr. Griffen [of the White Plains, N.Y., ration board], and a woman took his place before the desk. She said, rather archly, 'My dear Mr. Griffen, is this where you ration everything?'
>
> 'Everything but the ladies, Madam,' Mr. Griffen said gallantly. 'The government hasn't let us do that yet.'
>
> The woman fluttered her eyelids. Evidently everything was going to be just as she had hoped it would be. 'Well, I've an A card,' she said, 'but I think I deserve better. You see, my dear mother's eighty, and she's had a stroke. The only real pleasure she gets out of life is a little ride every evening . . . I'm afraid we won't be able to take our little rides unless you give me a B-3 card, or perhaps an X.'
>
> His air of gallantry still intact, Mr. Griffen said, 'I happen to have a mother, too, who's over eighty . . . But she'll have to make a certain number of sacrifices, just like the rest of us. She'll have to manage on an A card.'
>
> The woman stopped smiling. 'But, of course, an A card isn't enough,' she said. 'It may be the death of my poor mother.'
>
> 'All right,' Mr. Griffen said, standing up as a hint that the interview was about over. 'You go out and get an affidavit from your mother's physician swearing that unless she can ride a minimum of forty or fifty miles a week, every week, she'll die. Then you can come back here and get more gas.'
>
> —Brendan Gill, *The New Yorker,* June 13, 1942

K. CHESTER

Members of a Citizens Defense Corps dawn patrol in New York City's Harlem perform a drill, dousing a rooftop incendiary as the sun rises.

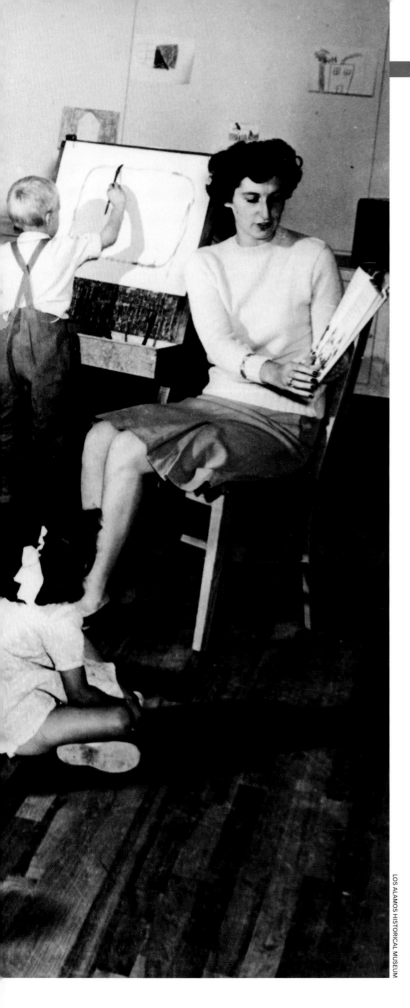

One school, Central (left), serves all Los Alamos employees' children. Oppenheimer and Maj. Gen. Leslie Groves (right) view the remains of a steel tower that held the first atom bomb tested.

UPI/CORBIS-BETTMANN

LOS ALAMOS HISTORICAL MUSEUM

" From university to university [Robert Oppenheimer] went, his pipe sending off plumes of smoke, his trench coat flapping and his new pork pie hat ... slanted forward against an imaginary wind. He was asking the best creative scientists he could find available to pick up their wives and children and live for a few years in the mountains ...

They came singly and in pairs and then virtually by the dozen, mostly young men with pony-tail wives and often babes in arms. Fourth generation Americans were intermingled with recent emigrants from Europe ... One day they were at home tending the garden ... the next day they had disappeared, sometimes traveling under assumed names and all bound for [Los Alamos] New Mexico where their address would simply be Box 1663, Santa Fe. "

—Peter Michelmore, *The Swift Years*

HANSEL MIETH AND OTTO HAGEL

ALFRED EISENSTAEDT

After Marine Capt. Marion Carl (left) brought down his 16th Japanese plane in the Solomons, he came home to raise public support for the war, addressing aircraft workers and selling bonds. He also met and married Edna Kirvin of Brooklyn, N.Y., and brought her to visit his family's farm near Hubbard, Oreg. Most soldiers and sailors (right) on furlough find that the folks at home are eager to hear, and even swap, war stories.

Furlough Greetings:

'So *you're* what's defending me!'

'You've certainly filled out since you got in the Army. You must get awfully good food.'

'How come you've been in nine months and only one stripe?'

'Gee, I wish I was in your shoes. They wouldn't take me on account of my eyes.'

'You can be a lot of help to me while you're here. The cook just quit.'

'I don't see why you don't write more often, with all the free time you boys have.'

'You young fellows are lucky. If I wasn't an old man with a family, I'd volunteer in a minute.'

'I don't see why you want to go out with that girl tonight. After all, we haven't seen you in six months.'

'I saw your old girl friend out dancing the other night. She was with a lieutenant.'

'The Army will be a good thing for you. It'll teach you to obey orders.'

—T5g. James P. Charles, *Yank*

Internees at a Japanese relocation center at Heart Mountain, Wyo., saluting the flag in −18° weather.

Right: Fumiko Hayashida and her one-year-old daughter, Natalie, are being relocated.

HANSEL MIETH

SEATTLE POST-INTELLIGENCER COLLECTION, MUSEUM OF HISTORY & INDUSTRY

" The resettlement center is actually a penitentiary—armed guards in towers with spotlights and deadly tommy guns, 15 feet of barbed-wire fences, everyone confined to quarters at nine, lights out at 10 o'clock. The guards are ordered to shoot anyone who approaches within 20 feet of the fences. No one is allowed to take the two-block-long hike to the latrines after nine, under any circumstances . . .

The food and sanitation problems are the worst. We have had absolutely no fresh meat, vegetables or butter since we came here . . . Stinking mud and slops everywhere.

Can this be the same America we left a few weeks ago? "

—Ted Nakashima,
The New Republic, June 15, 1942

THE LONELY

As Time Goes By

This day and age we're living in
Gives cause for apprehension,
With speed and new invention,
And things like third dimension,
Yet, we get a trifle weary,
With Mister Einstein's the'ry,
So we must get down to earth,
At times relax, relieve the tension.
No matter what the progress,
Or what may yet be proved,
The simple facts of life are such
They cannot be removed.

You must remember this,
A kiss is still a kiss, a sigh is just a sigh;
The fundamental things apply,
As time goes by.
And when two lovers woo,
They still say, "I love you,"
On that you can rely;
No matter what the future brings,
As time goes by.

Moonlight and love songs
Never out of date,
Hearts full of passion,
Jealousy and hate;
Woman needs man
And man must have his mate,
That no one can deny.
It's still the same old story,
A fight for love and glory,
A case of do or die!
The world will always welcome lovers,
As time goes by.
—*Lyric and music by Herman Hupfeld*

DMITRI KESSEL

JERRY COOKE

Pfc. James King (opposite) writes home from the Aleutians. Martha Jean Kuhn, 19, reads and rereads her letter from Capt. Dick Davisson, who is flying missions from England. To bolster her spirits, she wears the party dress that is his favorite.

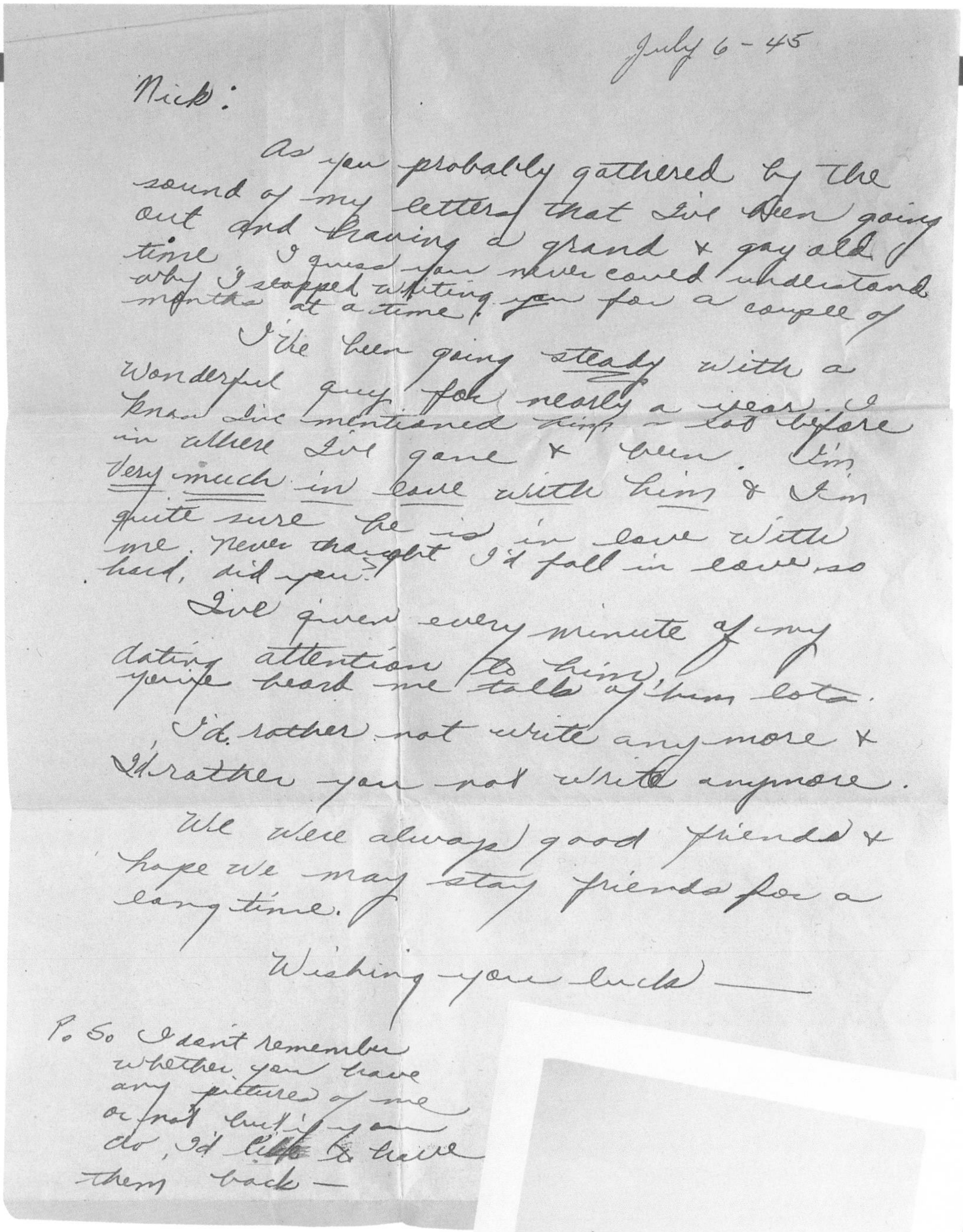

July 6 - 45

Nick:

As you probably gathered by the sound of my letters that I've been going out and having a grand & gay old time. I guess you never could understand why I stopped writing you for a couple of months at a time.

I've been going steady with a wonderful guy for nearly a year. I know I've mentioned him a lot before in where I've gone & been. I'm very much in love with him & I'm quite sure he is in love with me. Never thought I'd fall in love so hard, did you?

I've given every minute of my dating attention to him, you've heard me talk of him lots.

I'd rather not write anymore & I'd rather you not write anymore.

We were always good friends & hope we may stay friends for a long time.

Wishing you luck ———

P. S. I don't remember whether you have any pictures of me or not but if you do, I'd like to have them back ———

Seaman Marshall Nichols (on the right) is well along in his recovery from a "Dear John" letter.

" Nick:

As you probably gathered by the sound of my letters that I've been going out and having a grand & gay old time. I guess you never could understand why I stopped writing you for a couple of months at a time.

I've been going steady with a wonderful guy for nearly a year. I know I've mentioned him a lot before in where I've gone & been. I'm very much in love with him and I'm quite sure he is in love with me. Never thought I'd fall in love so hard, did you?

I've given every minute of my dating attention to him, ———, you've heard me talk of him lots.

I'd rather not write anymore & I'd rather you not write anymore.

We were always good friends & hope we may stay friends for a long time.

Wishing you luck—

P.S. I don't remember whether you have any pictures of me or not but if you do, I'd like to have them back— "

A PHOTOGRAPH OF YOU

When the evening shadows gather,
After all my work is thru,
I can't keep my eyes from straying,
To a photograph of you.

There it rests upon my table,
Just the way you looked that day,
Ah! It seems it was but yesterday,
When I first heard you say.

Words of love that made me happy,
and made all my dreams come true,
But — tonight, I'm all alone with
Just a photograph of you.

For one day our country called you
And you so bravely answered "here"
O h! I'm pround of you, my soldier,
Yet I brush away a tear -

Cause I miss your cheery whistle,
Miss your footsteps onethe stairs,
Miss your strong xxx arms and your kisses,
That can banish all my cares.

Then I wonder if your lonely--
Yes, I know you miss me too,
While I sit here dreaming--gazing,
At that photograph of you.

So I tiptoe to my window,
Kneel and wish upon a star
As I pray to God to keep you safe,
No matter where you are.

Thus my heart is ever with you
While I wait the long days thru,
And the dearest of all my treasures,
Is that photograph of you.

When the years have told their story
And the world is once more free,
I'll be waiting for you--darling
There will still be you and me.

Then we'll build our dreams together,
Hand in hand the long years thru,
But forever in my heart I'll hold
That photograph of you.

Beatrice Lutzin, 21, of New York City composed this poem and sent it to her boyfriend of four years, Sgt. Irving Simpson (below), 22, stationed in Biak, Dutch East Indies.

> Dear Jean,
> So the little 'whooping cough' bug caught up with you. Do be a brave girl and take your medicine . . .
>
> Did you have a cake for your birthday? How many of the candles did you blow out the first time? . . .
>
> I miss you very much. Let's pretend tonight that I'm there to get a good night hug & kiss from you. Remember me in your prayers.
> Daddy

—Maj. George Fisher, U.S. Army, to his daughter, September 19, 1941

Whether powering jump ropes or maneuvering small troops, American soldiers in England try to make up for time they are not able to spend with their own children.

Happiness brightens S2c. Louis A. Woisard as, unable to get home for the weekend, he talks with his folk in Danielson, Conn.

ALFRED EISENSTAEDT (10)

Surprise registers on the countenance of Pvt. Paul Willison as he talks from the phone center to his wife in Kalamazoo, Mich.

Delight is spread all over the face of S1c. Clarence H. Causey, USCGR, as he gets a home report from his wife in Asheboro, N.C.

Jocularity floods Motor Machinist Mate 2c. Howard McKenzie as he chats with his sister-in-law back at his home in Spartanburg, S.C.

Wistfulness lengthens the face of Pvt. James R. Lewis while he talks with his wife, Ruth, back in Centralia, Mo.

Paternal pride comes over S1c. G.S. Moffatt as his four-year-old son in Kenton, Tenn., talks about the last time his father left home.

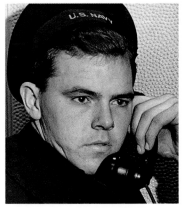

Faraway look comes into the eyes of S1c. Arthur Maynard, North Brookfield, Mass., calling his girl in Worcester.

Fond look covers the face of Pvt. Philip Schwab as he hears his two-year-old son in Chicago tell him, "I love you, Daddy."

Pleasure exudes from S1c. John Mains, talking to his mother in Chicago. They talk so often, center operators know her too.

> " More than a year ago the New York Telephone Company set up in Times Square the world's biggest telephone center for servicemen. It selected the crowded spot in New York City because servicemen pouring into Times Square for amusement found themselves lonesome for familiar voices and clogged the district's telephone booths with long-distance calls. An average of 700 men a day have since telephoned families and friends in every state, Canada, Brazil, Cuba, Curaçao and Hawaii and filled the center with the poignant drama of the wanderer long gone from home. "
>
> —LIFE, December 25, 1944

" Two GI's on the loose in London at a time when the GI uniform was still rare enough to stare at. They were AWOL for a weekend but the hell with it. The price was right.

If the beer was warm, so were the women.

They saw their first sign of war in the bleak mass of rubble behind Fleet Street, and it hit them hard.

They joined the unquenchable merry mood of men in a pub . . .

They walked into the awesome Westminster Abbey and the Houses of Parliament and London Bridge as if they were small boys turning the pages of a history book.

They admired the English accent of a Chinese waiter, the perfect cocktails in a posh club, the lovely lilt of a Gilbert and Sullivan operetta, the tucked-away scatter of pocket parks lined with ancient walls, the odd-shaped houses on tiny intertwining streets, the long queues of patient people, and the calm courage in their faces.

And when it was all over, they returned quietly to their camp in the Midlands, prepared to spend the next year on KP—only to discover that, in the confusion of their still-disorganized camp, nobody had even missed them. "

—Ralph G. Martin, *The GI War*

London's Hyde Park is the favored haunt for a GI and his English girlfriend (in this case, a member of the Auxiliary Territorial Service, part of the British Army).

FIGHTERS

"The highest honor
I have ever attained
is that of having my name
coupled with yours
in these great events."
—Gen. George S. Patton,
to the men of the
Third Army, 1945

As Allied forces embarked on the D-Day invasion, General Eisenhower invoked "the blessing of Almighty God upon this great and noble undertaking."

IMPERIAL WAR MUSEUM

> On a hospital ship bound for France:
> Two tired, brave, tough girls sat on a bench inside the hall of the ship, and painted their fingernails with bright red varnish . . .
>
> One of the British ship's officers . . . came to talk with the girls. He looked tired, too, and he was vastly amused by their nail polish. 'It would be nice,' he said, 'if we could take that nail polish up to London tonight, instead of where we're going.'
>
> The tall pretty nurse held her hands out to see whether the job was well done. 'No,' she said. She was from Texas and spoke in a soft, slow voice. 'No. I'm glad to be going just where I'm going. Don't you know how happy those little old boys are going to be when they see us coming?'
> —Martha Gellhorn, *Collier's,* August 5, 1944

Nurses (above) and soldiers on their way to the U.K.; an American troopship (opposite) nears the Algerian coast.

AP/WIDE WORLD PHOTOS

A National Fire Service girl (above) lights a doughboy's cigarette in London. Mrs. Hale (right), whose husband is fighting in France, spends her days giving the troops tea and refreshments in front of her house.

> When the American Army of Occupation (as British wags now call it) first reached these Isles, thoughtful men of both nations foresaw difficulties. Newspaper editorials, radio broadcasts and pamphlets warned of Anglo-American differences. Americans were advised they might find the British reserved and shy. Britons were told they would think Americans loudmouthed and arrogant. Both parties have been agreeably surprised. For the British public has been impressed by the good manners and discipline of U.S. troops. And Americans literally have been bowled over by the hospitality of British hosts.

—File from the *Time* and LIFE London bureau, 1942

FIGHTERS

The best equipped and most carefully trained riflemen in the world are those of the U.S. Army. So thoroughly did our troops understand the use and handling of their Springfields in World War I that they got more results per round of ammunition than any army had ever achieved. Today, with the more rapid-firing and compact Garand, they are preparing to beat their old record.

To improve training, the Army is considering the use of high-speed pictures, like the ones shown on these pages. **"**
—LIFE, September 21, 1942

GJON MILI (4)

Soldiers must learn to run with rifles ready to fire. As it is carried here, rifle can be brought forward and fired quickly from shoulder.

Correct way to fall forward while advancing under fire is shown here. Rifle is thrown ahead of body, kept in the air until soldier is horizontal.

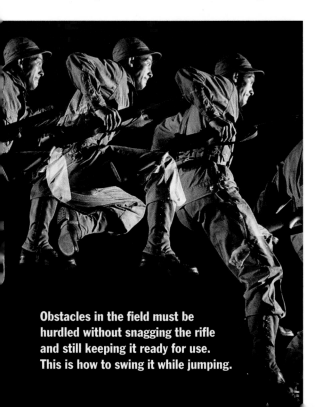

Obstacles in the field must be hurdled without snagging the rifle and still keeping it ready for use. This is how to swing it while jumping.

This is how to spring up for an advance. The soldier holds his rifle at its center, so that its weight is evenly distributed as he runs to the attack.

CULVER PICTURES

CORBIS/UPI/BETTMANN

Each soldier, sailor, Marine or airman has a unique story. Pfc. Wayne Nassi (above), for example, is a former jockey who weighed just 98 pounds when he entered the Army.

DON ORNITZ/GLOBE PHOTOS

> [Infantrymen] are rough and their language gets coarse because they live a life stripped of convention and niceties. Their nobility and dignity come from the way they live unselfishly and risk their lives to help each other . . . There are gentlemen and boors; intelligent ones and stupid ones; talented ones and inefficient ones. But when they are all together and they are fighting, despite their bitching and griping and goldbricking and mortal fear, they are facing cold steel and screaming lead and hard enemies, and they are advancing and beating the hell out of the opposition.
>
> —Bill Mauldin, *Up Front*

W. EUGENE SMITH

NATIONAL ARCHIVES

JOHNNY FLOREA

Infantrymen (above) advance into a Belgian town. Medic (right) helps retrieve a man wounded when two U.S. tanks were knocked out by landmines near Aachen, Germany.

" It is a bad time for fighting. The nights are freezing cold, the rain seldom lets up, the battlefields are oceans of mud . . .

The stakes of the winter battle are large and the losses are bound to be heart-rending. As the casualty lists come in, let responsible citizens remember that in another war Lincoln and Grant were driven to an almost similar decision: to commit everything the nation had to the ending of the struggle and the preservation of the Union. "

—LIFE, December 11, 1944

Sergeants George McGray of Somerville, Mass., and Bernard Haber of New York City stop to read a map in Tunisia's unfamiliar terrain. American soldiers in the North African campaign were inexperienced in desert warfare but learned from the British.

ELIOT ELISOFON

> Mollie was the biggest popoff and the biggest screwball and the biggest foul-up I ever saw, and he wasn't afraid of nothing. Some fellows get brave with experience, I guess, but Mollie never had any fear to begin with. Like one time on the road to Maknassy, the battalion was trying to take some hills and we were getting no place . . . Mollie stands right up . . . 'I bet those Italians would surrender if somebody asked them to. What the hell do they want to fight for?' he says. So he walks across the minefield

U.S. troops march toward strategic Troina, in Sicily.

and up the hill to the Italians, waving his arms and making funny motions, and they shoot at him for a while and then stop, thinking he is crazy ... When he gets to the Italians he finds a soldier who was a barber in Astoria but went home on a visit and got drafted in the Italian Army, so the barber translates for him and the Italians say sure, they would like to surrender, and Mollie comes back to the lines with 568 prisoners.

—A.J. Liebling, *The New Yorker,* June 2, 1945

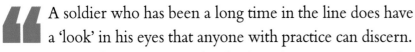

Left: After the siege of a German town, infantryman Stephen Longstreth has his first hot meal in 15 days.

Right: Cpl. Frank Johnson of Brooklyn rests at a forward supply point in France.

CULVER PICTURES (2)

> **"** A soldier who has been a long time in the line does have a 'look' in his eyes that anyone with practice can discern. It's a look of dullness, eyes that look without seeing, eyes that see without transferring any response to the mind. It's a look that is the display room for the thoughts that lie behind it— exhaustion, lack of sleep, tension for too long, weariness that is too great, fear beyond fear, misery to the point of numbness, a look of surpassing indifference to anything anybody can do to you. It's a look I dread to see on men. **"**
>
> —Ernie Pyle, April 5, 1944

> In U.S. underground facilities, Corregidor: A corpsman came into General Moore's office, tears streaming down his face. He sobbed out what we all knew: 'There's a white flag waving at the hospital tunnel entrance.'
>
> To most, the surrender [on May 6, 1942] came as a relief. But the silence following the surrender was worse than the shelling. It was uncanny, awful. The sudden opening of a door, a falling chair, would make us jump and flinch. In the moment of surrender none of us thought of tomorrow, for there was no tomorrow. For us, the end had come.
>
> —Lt. Col. S.M. Mellnik, LIFE, February 7, 1944

U.S. soldiers (above) surrender to the Japanese at Corregidor in the Philippines. American POWs (left) in a camp on Mindanao, at great risk and in defiance of their captors, observe the Fourth of July in 1942.

Left: Paratroopers in France, about to jump into Germany, have had special haircuts for luck and esprit de corps. Opposite: A fallen tree on Guadalcanal provides an outpost for bathing and doing laundry.

ROBERT CAPA/MAGNUM PHOTOS

> " The yarning went on, and finally somebody told the classic story about the two Marine jeep drivers on Guadalcanal, supposedly a true story . . . about two jeeps passing in the night, one with proper dim-out headlights, the other with glaring bright lights. So the driver of the dim-light car leans out as they pass and shouts to the other driver: 'Hey! Put your f-----g lights out!' To which the other replies: 'I can't. I've got a f-----g colonel with me!' "
>
> —Richard Tregaskis, *Guadalcanal Diary*

RALPH MORSE

W. EUGENE SMITH

AP/WIDE WORLD PHOTOS

One Marine offers a smoke to a prisoner on Iwo Jima (above), while others (right) blow up a cave that sheltered Japanese soldiers.

> It is in situations like this that Marine Corps training proves its value. There probably wasn't a man among us who didn't wish to God he was moving in the opposite direction. But ... pride helped now to keep us from faltering. Few of us would have admitted that we were bound by the old-fashioned principle of 'death before dishonor' but it was probably this, above all else, that kept us pressing forward.
> —Gerald Astor, *The Greatest War*

Injured rear gunner Kenneth Bratton (above) is pulled from the turret of his Avenger aboard the USS *Saratoga*. Lieutenant Walter Chewning (right) races to the aid of a pilot crash-landing on the USS *Enterprise*.

" Suddenly, U.S. ships faced the onslaught of the 'divine wind'— kamikaze attacks. From October 1944 until war's end, 1,228 Japanese pilots dove to their deaths, sinking 30 U.S. ships and damaging 288. 'We were always on edge,' remembers Frank Albert, a ship fitter. 'Once, during a cowboy movie on the hangar deck, a bugle sounded, and within seconds the area was cleared as men scrambled to battle stations. A minute later an announcement recalled us to our seats. The bugle call was in the movie.' "

—World War II (LIFE special issue)

NATIONAL ARCHIVES

CULVER PICTURES

Cadets in training line up for review (above) at the Tuskegee Institute in Alabama. Pilots of the 332nd Fighter Group, 15th Air Force, in Italy (right) gather in the shadow of one of the North American P-51s they fly.

"Displaying outstanding courage, aggressiveness, and combat technique, the group immediately engaged the enemy formation in aerial combat . . . Through their superior skill and determination, the group destroyed three enemy aircraft, probably destroyed three and damaged three . . . with no losses sustained by the 332nd Fighter Group . . . By the conspicuous gallantry, professional skill, and determination of the pilots, together with the outstanding technical skill and devotion to duty of the ground personnel, the 332nd Fighter Group has reflected great credit on itself and the armed forces of the United States."

—Distinguished Unit Citation, October 16, 1945

" Major James Stewart returned to his base today after leading all Liberators on the Brunswick raid and said, smilingly, 'It was all right.' Asked if he saw any German planes, the former Hollywood star, now a squadron commander, replied, 'Not one.'

He said his ship ran into some anti-aircraft fire over the target and around the Netherland coast, but 'our fighter escort is the best I've ever seen' . . . It was the first time Major Stewart had commanded such a big flight of four-engined bombers, and fellow-airmen pointed out that his selection for the job was recognition of his flying ability. On previous raids Major Stewart, as squadron commander, led a group of 20 or more Liberators. Today's was his 10th mission, earning an Oak Leaf Cluster for the Air Medal he received after five missions. **"**

—*The New York Times,* March 1, 1944

Major James M. Stewart (above), in England, reviews final details before squadron members take off on a bombing mission. Captain Clark Gable (right), also in England, is a gunnery instructor and has seen action over Germany.

CORBIS-BETTMANN

" To the combat soldier, in the end, nothing held greater importance than comradeship. Indeed, as protracted campaigning darkened and dirtied everything else, it provoked an intensification of comradeship. 'Friendship,' said Eugene Sledge, 'was the only comfort a man had.' Comradeship—friends' love and loyalty and devotion to one another—seemed the only redeeming presence in war; it alone was able to sustain a world in which battle had reduced their consciousness to 'us.' As Kurt Gabel [said,] 'We would march in step for *us,* sing for *us,* excel for *us,* endure for *us* and ... suffer and die for *us.* For each other.' "

—Gerald F. Linderman
The World Within War

Submariners share a relaxed cup of coffee in port before setting out to sea. "Submarine men," explains one commander, "have a deep inner feeling, not always shared by their officers, that everything by grace of God will turn out all right."

U.S. ARMY SIGNAL CORPS

A moment of rest for crewmen (left) aboard a new light cruiser and for 1st Sgt. Rance Richardson (right) of Lockesburg, Ark., who also fought in the First World War.

"Dear YANK:
Here is a question that each Negro soldier is asking. What is the Negro soldier fighting for? On whose team are we playing? Myself and eight other soldiers were on our way from Camp Claiborne, La., to the hospital here at Fort Huachuca. We had to lay over until the next day for our train. On the next day we could not purchase a cup of coffee at any of the lunchrooms around there. As you know, Old Man Jim Crow rules.

The only place where we could be served was at the lunchroom at the railroad station but, of course, we had to go into the kitchen. But that's not all; 11:30 a.m. about two dozen German prisoners of war, with two American guards, came to the station. They entered the lunchroom, sat at the tables, had their meals served, talked, smoked, in fact had quite a swell time.

I stood on the outside looking on, and I could not help but ask myself these questions: Are these men sworn enemies of this country? Are they not taught to hate and destroy . . . all democratic governments? Are we not American soldiers, sworn to fight for and die if need be for this our country? Then why are they treated better than we are? Why are we pushed around like cattle? If we are fighting for the same thing, if we are to die for our country, then why does the Government allow such things to go on? Some of the boys are saying that you will not print this letter. I'm saying that you will."

—Cpl. Rupert Trimmingham
Fort Huachuca, Ariz., in *Yank*

FPG INTERNATIONAL

> **❝** There inside was this pathetic young mother with three other young children . . . dirt floor, a pile of dirty straw to sleep on, a small fire burning on the floor . . .
>
> Danny drove back to the base and then returned to this hut, all in about 30 minutes, but this time with C-rations, canned corned beef, canned sausage, powdered milk, chocolate bars, soap.
>
> He just left it there, and went away, didn't say anything. In five days he made five trips like that. **❞**
>
> —Fred Rochlin, *Old Man in a Baseball Cap*

A technician fifth grade shares his meal with Italian children (above); American soldiers (right) in Cherbourg examine captured German wine stores.

UNDERWOOD PHOTO ARCHIVES INC.

HULTON GETTY/LIAISON AGENCY

Seventh Army troops pose
atop a captured German
railroad gun (below),
and a single American soldier
(opposite) stands in a
bombed-out church in Italy.

"My best friend over there was an ardent Catholic. He used to pray and go to confession and Mass whenever he could. I kept telling him, 'What's the use? The whole business is written down in a book someplace. Praying won't make any difference.' But whenever I got caught in a tight spot over Germany, I'd find myself whispering, 'God, you gotta. You gotta get me back. God, listen, you gotta.'"
—Brendan Gill, *The New Yorker,* August 12, 1944

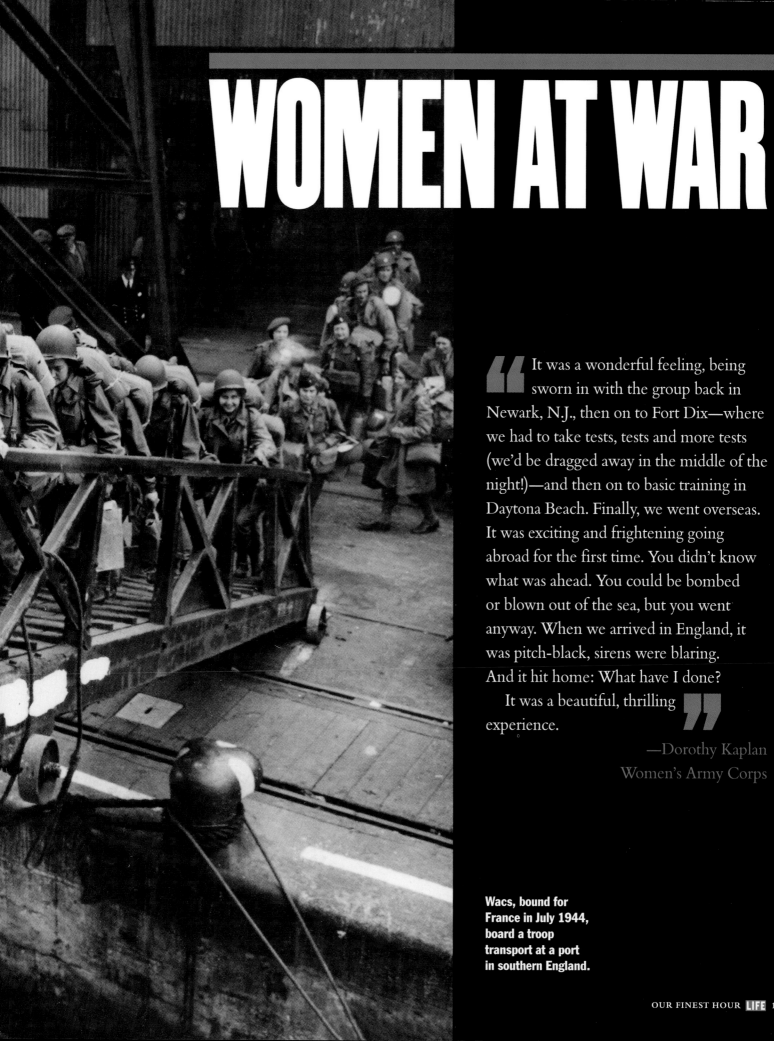

WOMEN AT WAR

“ It was a wonderful feeling, being sworn in with the group back in Newark, N.J., then on to Fort Dix—where we had to take tests, tests and more tests (we'd be dragged away in the middle of the night!)—and then on to basic training in Daytona Beach. Finally, we went overseas. It was exciting and frightening going abroad for the first time. You didn't know what was ahead. You could be bombed or blown out of the sea, but you went anyway. When we arrived in England, it was pitch-black, sirens were blaring. And it hit home: What have I done?

It was a beautiful, thrilling experience. ”

—Dorothy Kaplan
Women's Army Corps

Wacs, bound for France in July 1944, board a troop transport at a port in southern England.

" Boot camp consisted of six weeks of marching, saluting and learning, six weeks of training as hard as the men ... The women marched two and three hours without stopping to rest. 'If some girl fainted you were to step over her and go on, for if you stopped to help you got a demerit,' [said one recruit] ... The drill instructors were tartars. After shining her shoes for an hour, she would be told they were dirty. If a recruit forgot to button a button, it was roughly pulled off and handed to her. Hair was measured with a ruler to be sure it was the proper length ... The women hated the drill instructor but they did as he said. They learned that a Marine always follows orders. "

—Olga Gruhzit-Hoyt, *They Also Served*

Nurses (above) enroll in Seattle for possible military service. Women Marines (right) aboard a Coast Guard–manned transport in the Pacific stay in shape.

A church is pressed into service as a hospital in the Philippines (opposite). Nurses were among the first women to arrive at the Normandy beachhead after D-Day; one at left assists in the operating theater (right).

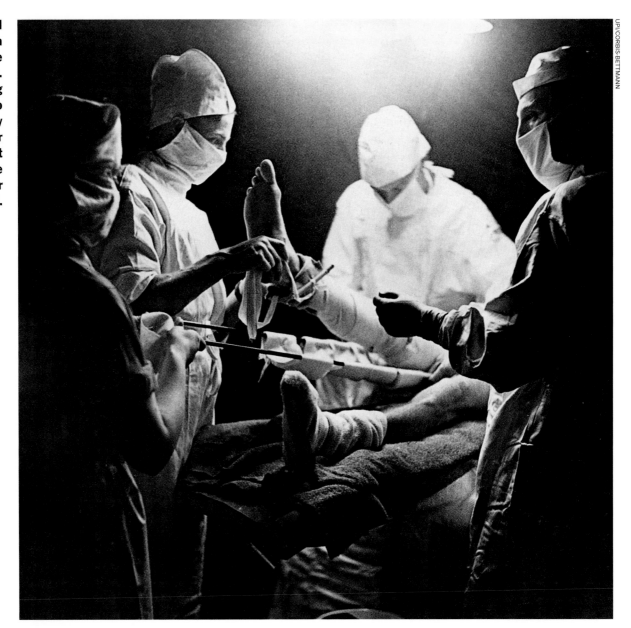

UPI/CORBIS-BETTMANN

W. EUGENE SMITH

" I can remember every case we ever had, especially the first one. The ambulance brought him in late one afternoon. I came over to where he was lying and he looked up and grinned. I asked him how he felt. He said something about the German with a machine pistol using him for a dart board. He was quiet and patient and a little bewildered. He'd never been hurt before. He asked how the fighting was going. Then he passed out.

The doctor came over and looked at his wounds and then swore, saying he had no business to be alive. We put him on the operating table and did what we could. The doctor kept swearing all the time he was operating. We couldn't stop the bleeding.

I remember the radio news that night: They said the casualties had been surprisingly light. "

—Military nurse, *The True Glory* (War Department film)

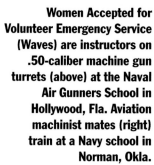

U.S. NAVY PHOTOGRAPH

UPI/CORBIS-BETTMANN

Women Accepted for Volunteer Emergency Service (Waves) are instructors on .50-caliber machine gun turrets (above) at the Naval Air Gunners School in Hollywood, Fla. Aviation machinist mates (right) train at a Navy school in Norman, Okla.

“ The point that Captain Mildred McAfee liked most to make was that her Waves had released more than 70,000 men for combat, which was the same as adding 70,000 men to the Navy's muster. They were the second largest women's service branch. The Coast Guard's SPARs numbered 9,745; the women Marines 19,000. There were 82,000 Waves in uniform and 92,500 Wacs. Considering the difference in size between the Army and Navy, women were carrying a proportionately far greater load in the Navy. ”

—*Time*, March 12, 1945

PETER STACKPOLE (3)

Women's Air Force Service Pilots (WASPs) ferry aircraft from factory to base, serve as test pilots and flight instructors, shuttle officers, tow targets for artillery practice. Here, pilot trainees at Avenger Field, near Sweetwater, Tex.: Letter writer Madge Rutherford (left) waits for her flight period; Rebecca Edwards (below, left) is, at 22, already a war widow.

" Dear Mrs. Roosevelt,
Would the Civil Aeronautics Authority charter a reserve air corps for women? . . . Approximately 487 girls received flight training under the C.A.A. private pilot training program during this past school year . . . Like the other 486 girls, I have wind in my veins . . . Mrs. Roosevelt, could you help us? "

—Madge Rutherford

" Dear Miss Rutherford:
Mrs. Roosevelt has requested that we make direct reply to your letter . . . no discrimination will be made against pilots of your sex. "

—Civil Aeronautics Authority

ENTERTAINERS

> "Most impressive of all the feats of Marlene the doer-of-good-deeds was her three years of wartime work entertaining American troops, from the Anzio beachhead to Greenland and the Aleutians. Marlene herself calls it 'the only important thing I've ever done.' She worked far from publicity cameras and often perilously near the front lines. Bundled in a couple of GI overcoats, her hands often freezing, standing patiently in chow lines with her mess kit, sleeping in rat-infested ruins and dugouts, Trouper Dietrich put on a performance that was a triumph of sheer stamina. GIs remember her setting her shoulder to an overturned jeep in Italy, helping a pair of French army officers to right it. She got virus pneumonia in Bari. She had a close call among retreating troops at the Battle of the Bulge. She entered Rome with the American troops, performing on the back of a truck."
>
> —LIFE, August 18, 1952

GEORGE SILK

Dietrich delights servicemen near the front with the "mental telepathy" portion of her act, in which she turns her back to them and then, unfailingly, tells them what they are thinking.

I Left My Heart at the Stage Door Canteen

Old Mister Absentminded, that's me.
Just as forgetful as I can be.
I've got the strangest sort of a mind.
I'm always leaving something behind.

I left my heart at the stage door
    canteen.
I left it there with a girl named Eileen.
I kept her serving doughnuts 'til all she
    had were gone.
I sat there dunking doughnuts 'til she
    caught on.
I must go back to the Army routine.
And ev'ry doughboy knows what that
    will mean.
A soldier boy without a heart
Has two strikes on him from the start
And my heart's at the stage door
    canteen.

—*Music and lyric by Irving Berlin*

Pvt. Ed Maron and actress Dorothy McGuire at New York City's Stage Door Canteen.

A Quonset hut on Adak, a vital U.S. base in the Aleutians

DMITRI KESSEL

BOB LANDRY

This picture ran in 1941; LIFE got letters.

" Sirs:
Henceforth our bugler agrees to blow reveille 15 minutes late, giving us more time to dream of Rita Hayworth.
PFC. HOWARD A. FLEMING (DREAMER)
PVT. HAROLD D. GANN (BUGLER)
Fort Warren, Wyo.
P.S. Wow!

Sirs:
Wow!
GENE M. KRONBERG
Philadelphia

Sirs:
Wow!!!
GEORGE A. KIMBALL
Kearny, N.J. **"**

> **LIFE** asked Ginger Rogers to give a dream
> party for a GI. Ginger asked seven other girls to
> come to her Beverly Hills home and help out. You
> probably know them—from movies or from pin-ups.
> Pvt. John Farnsworth, who served three years in the
> Pacific and is home recovering from malaria, was
> also glad to come. The girls fed Private Farnsworth,
> listened to him, admired him, danced with him, played
> games with him. It was a very enjoyable party.
> But don't count on its ever happening to you.
>
> —LIFE, September 25, 1944

Private Farnsworth blushed when meeting (top, clockwise from left) Barbara Hale, Lynne Baggett, Gloria DeHaven, Lynn Bari, Jinx Falkenburg, Dolores Moran, Chili Williams and Ginger. They treated him like a king, then sent the 22-year-old veteran on his way with colorful kisses.

HART PRESTON

NATIONAL BASEBALL LIBRARY

Sergeant Joe Louis (left) launches a 100-day coast-to-coast goodwill tour. Sergeant Joe DiMaggio (above) of the Army Air Force shoulders a bat for enthusiastic fans.

" To those who remember the tongue-tied, taciturn title-winner of six years ago, Joe Louis's present personality is a revelation of what metamorphoses public life and Army life can work. Affable and at home on his feet, he gives a gracious and fluent talk on physical fitness and how to be a good soldier. He responds quickly and good-humoredly to unceasing questions fired at him by soldier fans. The most frequent question was, 'How much do you weigh now?' Answer: 'Just 215. That's 10 pounds over my fighting weight.' Question: 'Who's the hardest puncher you ever fought?' Answer: 'Max Baer, but he never hit me.'

There is no doubt that Joe's trip has proved a success from its inception. And in it many find not only educational and morale-building values but also a quiet parable in racial goodwill. "

—LIFE, September 13, 1943

Major (and bandleader) Glenn Miller (above, left) was reported missing in December 1944 after his plane disappeared. The Andrews Sisters (left) welcome homecoming troops.

> We sang 'Don't Sit Under the Apple Tree' . . . 'Don't go walking down Lovers' Lane
> With anyone else but me
> Till I come marching home.'
> The scene [in Seattle] is still vivid in my memory. We stood down on the pier, looking up at all those young men leaning over the ship's rails, waving and yelling and screaming . . . All over the country in 1942, one thought nagged at you: How many of the young men shipping out wouldn't come back?
>
> —Maxene Andrews and Bill Gilbert
> *Over Here, Over There*

BUY MORE BONDS

PHOTOFEST

KATHRYN KRULL

Singer Kate Smith (above) opened a new booth for the Treasury Department and bought a $50,000 bond herself. Carole Lombard (right) demonstrates in Indianapolis how much Hollywood talent has helped the war effort.

" Late on January 16 movie actress Carole Lombard was killed in a plane crash high in the mountains east of the Sierra Nevada. The previous day, in a few exhausting hours, she had sold $2,017,531 worth of Defense Bonds and Stamps.

At four a.m., Miss Lombard boarded the TWA plane at Indianapolis Airport. She had been strongly urged to return to Hollywood by rail, but had found herself unable to face three days on the 'choo-choo train.' Her plane was not a sleeper, but she didn't mind sitting up. 'When I get home,' said Miss Lombard, 'I'll flop in bed and sleep for 12 hours.' Thirty-six hours later searchers reached the wreckage where her body lay. "

—LIFE, January 26, 1942

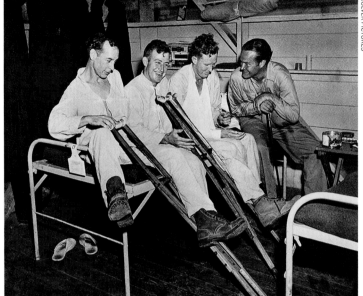

> In a hospital for war wounded:
> Hope and company had worked and gradually they got the leaden eyes to sparkling, had planted and nurtured and coaxed laughter to life . . . Finally it came time for Frances Langford to sing. The men asked for 'As Time Goes By' . . . She got through eight bars and was into the bridge, when a boy with a head wound began to cry. She stopped, and then went on, but her voice wouldn't work any more, and she finished the song whispering and then she walked out, so no one could see her, and broke down. The ward was quiet and no one applauded. And then Hope walked into the aisle between the beds and he said seriously, 'Fellows, the folks at home are having a terrible time about eggs. They can't get any powdered eggs at all. They've got to use the old-fashioned kind that you break open.'
> There's a man for you—there really is a man.
> —John Steinbeck, *Once There Was a War*

Bob Hope and Frances Langford (left) bring their USO show to North Africa. Hope (above) visits with wounded soldiers in the South Pacific.

THE WOUNDED

"One Fourth Division soldier in Huertgen . . . stepped on a mine and blew off his foot . . .

The man lay there, but he wasn't able to bandage his own wounds. The medics tried to reach him but were fired upon. One was hit, and the trees around the man were white with scars of the machine-gun bullets that kept the medics away. Finally—after 70 hours—they managed to reach him.

He was still conscious, and for the medics it was a blessing that he was conscious; and for the man himself it was a blessing. For during the darkness the Germans had moved up to the wounded man. They took his field jacket from him, and his cigarettes. They booby-trapped him by setting a charge under his back, so that whoever lifted him would die. So the wounded man, knowing this, lay quietly on the charge and told the men who came to help him what the Germans had done. They cut the wires of the booby trap and carried him away.

—Mack Morriss, *Yank*, January 5, 1945

A wounded soldier awaits evacuation from Okinawa in April 1945.

LIFE followed George Lott on a 4,500-mile odyssey through three field dressing stations and five hospitals in France and England, then home to the U.S. Left: one hour after his wounding on November 22; below: help with a smoke; right: receiving a second plaster cast on December 14 (the first was removed so penicillin could be applied to his wounds).

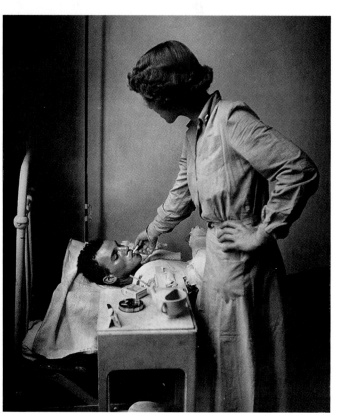

“ George Lott, 22, a medical soldier, exposed himself to fire in an attempt to answer the call of a wounded man. Fragments of a German shell ripped into both his arms as he made his way 500 yards on foot back to his own battalion aid station in the cellar of a house in the village. There he first reported to his medical officer the location of two casualties whose wounds he had dressed. Then, stunned and numbed but still on his feet, he submitted his own grievous wounds to treatment. 'Doc,' he said, 'I feel like both my arms were blown off.' ”

—LIFE, January 29, 1945

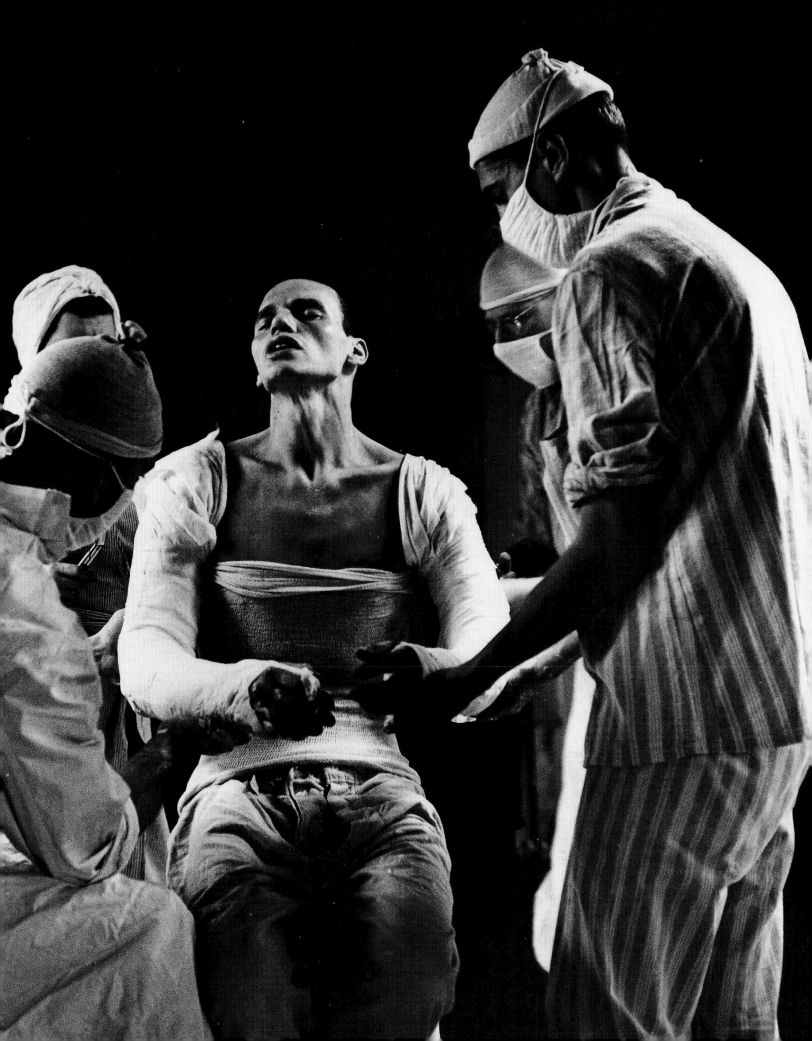

> " A man lay on his back in the small space of the upside-down cockpit . . . His left leg was broken and punctured by an ack-ack burst. His back was terribly burned by raw gasoline that had spilled. The foot of his injured leg was pinned rigidly under the rudder bar.
>
> His space was so small he couldn't squirm around to relieve his own weight from his paining back. He couldn't straighten out his legs, which were bent above him. He couldn't see out of his little prison. He had not had a bite to eat or a drop of water. All this for eight days and nights . . .
>
> Our rescue party cussed as they worked, cussed with open admiration for [the] greatness of heart which had kept him alive and sane through his lonely and gradually hope-dimming ordeal. "
>
> —Ernie Pyle
> August 22, 1944

An injured flier is treated in the wreckage of his glider (opposite); a young private (right) holds a Purple Heart for wounds received when German guns shelled his hospital tent.

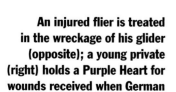

Santa visits Army and Marine hospitals on Guadalcanal, dispensing Red Cross presents and doing sailor dances in 90° temperatures on Christmas Day, 1943.

RALPH MORSE

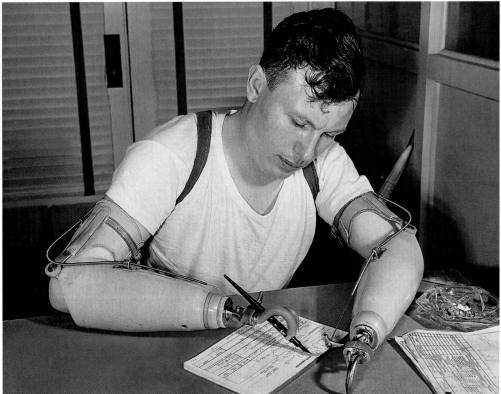

U.S. SIGNAL CORPS

Russell practices late into the night to conquer such formerly simple tasks as writing or drinking coffee. Hooks are opened by cords that are pulled across his back by the opposite shoulder.

U.S. SIGNAL CORPS (3)

" One way to break down the depression of those who have been permanently damaged by battle wounds is 'celluloid therapy,' showing with movies how another man overcame their problem. Such a movie is *Diary of a Sergeant,* a minor cinematic masterpiece made by the Signal Corps. The star is Sgt. Harold Russell, who preferred useful hooks to ornamental but useless artificial hands. "

—LIFE, July 23, 1945

It took three months of near starvation for a Nazi prisoner of war camp to reduce Private Demler to the state of ill health shown in LIFE's April 16, 1945, issue. Like many in the prison, he had become too weak to rise from his bed.

" Dear Sir:
Pvt. Joseph G. Demler, the former American prisoner of war whose photograph you ran in a recent issue [opposite], was evacuated by air to Mitchel Field [N.Y.] after his release. When your cameraman photographed him, Demler was down to 70 pounds as a result of Nazi callousness and brutality. But when he arrived at Mitchel he had already gained back 29 of the 80 pounds he had lost. In this picture, taken for the *Mitchel Beacon* by Cpl. Bernard Von Elm, Demler is looking at the LIFE picture, the first copy of the photograph he saw. "

—S. Sgt. Bert Briller
LIFE, June 11, 1945

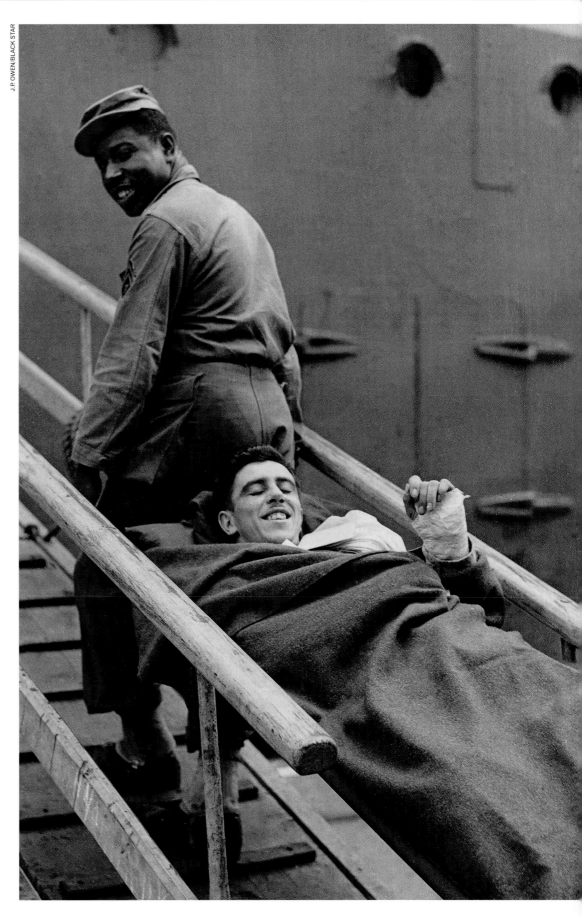

A wounded soldier bound for home

THE STORYTELLERS

LIFE photojournalist Jack Wilkes has at times traveled with writer Theodore White on war assignments. These—a Rolleiflex camera and a standard-issue portable typewriter—are the tools of his trade. The typewriter does double duty, as it also comes in handy for a letter home.

10

We finally beat our way back to Kunming in about 3 days of desperate driving and lucky airplane connections suffering only 2 flat tires. We didn't have any on the way down but we were just plain lucky. Most people who went down were getting anyplace from 5 to ten flats a day. The Railroad runs along the road for uite a spell in some places and when our boys worked over those trains puncture possibilities were scattered all over the road with shrapnell and all those other things they use in a shooting war....and when some innocent guy drives down the road months later he still gets shrapnel, right in the old innertube.

We were delayed for a couple of hours or so in one spot. One of these ramshackle bridges with the planks over the sampans was all busted up. A weapons carrier which is much heavier than a jeep tried to cross over it and broke the damned bridge and fouled up everything so we couldn't get across and had to wait until they nailed up a sampan as a ferry to get us across.

Teddy's quite a guy to have on these little junkets as he can really kick the Chinese language around. He had about a hours conversation ith the colonel who speaks no english much to the amusement and amasement of the GIs around our little happy home that we stayed while at the front. Teddy and myself get along pretty good as a team, In fact we can inter-change our clothing, (the bastards wearing a pair of my pants now) but I think he was a little suspicious of me at first. You're familiar with the usual Life Cameramens temperament so we have a couple of strikes against us in the first place. I suppose e was expecting the outburst of

HULTON-DEUTSCH/CORBIS

> I was addressed by the [French] guerrilla force as 'Captain' . . . But they were a little upset and worried by my very low rank, and one of them, whose trade for the past year had been receiving mines and blowing up German ammunition trucks and staff cars, asked confidentially, 'My Captain, how is it that with your age and your undoubted long years of service and your obvious wounds (caused by hitting a static water tank in London) you are still a captain?'
>
> 'Young man,' I told him, 'I have not been able to advance in rank due to the fact that I cannot read or write.'
>
> —Ernest Hemingway
> *Collier's,* September 30, 1944

War correspondent Ernest Hemingway (above) looks over his work. The war's best cartoon humorist, Sgt. Bill Mauldin (right), sketches in a town in Italy.

JOHN PHILLIPS

*"Just gimme th' aspirin.
I already got a Purple Heart."*

Somewhere in Italy:
It's a little difficult for me now to remember just when I first met Joe the infantryman. He didn't appear suddenly, and we were never formally introduced. He hung around for years and I suspect that, like Topsy, he just grew.

If Joe had any beginning at all it must have been back in 1940. I was a private in an infantry rifle company and so damn mad at my company commander and first sergeant and mess sergeant and corporal that I wanted to get even with them all.

After retreat, unless I had late KP, I would take off across the parade ground and spend half the night drawing nasty cartoons about the officers and mess sergeants for the division newspaper. Then I'd be sleepy and miss reveille next morning; the officers would have me where they wanted me until the day was over and I could go back and draw more cartoons.

—Bill Mauldin, LIFE, March 27, 1944

CBS's Edward R. Murrow
(right, in 1941) broadcast
from Blitz-torn London.
War reporter Ernie Pyle
(opposite) uses his helmet
for a footbath.

"Today I walked down a long street. The gutters were full of glass; the big red buses couldn't pull into the curb. There was the harsh, grating sound of glass being shoveled into trucks. In one window—or what used to be a window—was a sign. It read: SHATTERED—BUT NOT SHUTTERED . . . Halfway down the block there was a desk on the sidewalk; a man sat behind it with a pile of notes at his elbow. He was paying off the staff of the store—the store that stood there yesterday."

—Edward R. Murrow,
during the Blitz

" Ernie has come to be envisaged as a frail old poet, a kind of St. Francis of Assisi wandering sadly among the foxholes, playing beautiful tunes on his typewriter. Actually he is neither elderly, little, saintly nor sad. He is 44 years old; stands five feet eight inches tall; weighs 112 pounds; and though he appears fragile he is a tough, wiry man who gets along nicely without much food or sleep. His sense of humor, which leavens his columns with quaint chuckling passages, assumes a robust earthy color in conversation. His laugh is full-bellied. His profanity is strictly GI. His belch is internationally renowned. "

—LIFE, April 2, 1945

Photojournalists like Margaret Bourke-White (above), W. Eugene Smith (right) and Robert Capa (opposite) cover the war by subjecting themselves to the same stresses and situations faced by our combat forces in Europe, Africa and Asia.

" On D-Day: After an hour and a half my film was all used up and I saw a landing craft behind me with a lot of medics getting out and getting killed as they got out. I waited in the water for all the medics to get out and then I climbed aboard. Then I felt a slight shock and my eyes were all covered with feathers. I thought, 'What is this? Is somebody killing chickens?' Then I saw that the superstructure was shot away and the feathers were stuffing from the kapok jackets of men who had been killed. The skipper was crying because his assistant had been blown all over him and he was a mess. Then things got confused. I was very exhausted. Some men were giving transfusions to the wounded. An LCVP came for the wounded and I went with them. "

—Robert Capa
LIFE, June 26, 1944

THE LOST

Seaman Second Class Warren Harrell McCutcheon, 17, a sailor on the USS *Maryland,* perished in the attack.

"From Pearl Harbor:
The casualties were already pouring in. I did the first operation . . . in this war if that is anything. I spent the next 72 hours in four-hour shifts at the operating table. During my first shift we were under almost constant bombing and the [antiaircraft fire] kept up a constant din. They didn't actually hit the hospital but one explosion was so close it blew all the windows out . . . next to the room I was operating in . . . These poor devils brought in all shot up and burned. Many of them hopeless. We gave them plenty of morphine and sent them out in the wards to die. The others we patched up as best we could."

—Letter from Lt. Comdr. Paul Spangler, M.D., U.S. Navy, December 17, 1941

Sailors in Hawaii honor the memory of comrades lost six months earlier in the sneak attack on Pearl Harbor.

WILLIAM C. SHROUT (2)

Harrodsburg's birthday on June 16 is marked by a parade of Home Guardsmen (left). Arch Woods's store (right) shows pictures of the town's soldiers and sailors. Tags written by parents tell where their boys are serving.

"When Bataan fell on April 9, the Japanese captured 36,853 U.S. and Filipino troops. Among these were 66 men from Harrodsburg, Ky. (pop. 4,673). In a friendly town like Harrodsburg, where neighbors call each other by first name and have watched each other's boys grow up and put on their first long pants and graduate from school, the swallowing up of 66 of its young men in a single day is hard to bear. Even harder, in a way, is the lack of news about them—where they are, how they are doing, what they are getting to eat.

But Harrodsburg's people are showing their unbroken courage in many quiet ways. They have taken to putting snapshots of their sons in a Main Street store window for their friends to see. The day after Bataan fell almost every house in Harrodsburg put out a flag, and they are still out.

By the next Fourth of July the U.S. will have a great many Harrodsburgs. For until it does this war cannot be won."

—LIFE, July 6, 1942

Mrs. Ruth Graham (left) sorts possessions. Effects (below) arrive in bags, suitcases, trunks and ammunition boxes.

> In Kansas City, Mo., last week, as for weeks before and for many weeks to come, railroad cars were shunted alongside a former mail-order-company building and were emptied of their freight—the effects of U.S. soldiers killed or missing in action.
>
> In the Army Effects Bureau, the dead men's things are unpacked, sorted, packed again and sent to the soldiers' families. From this emptying of dead men's pockets come Bibles, prayer books, letters, snapshots, diaries. There are walrus tusks from men in the north, scarabs from men who died in Africa and souvenirs from all over. One boy carried a circular from a muscle-building company, still undecided as he went to his death whether he should buy the regulation 'chest-pull-and-barbell combination' at $5.95 or the 'super-strength set' at $6.95.
>
> The Effects Bureau is a quiet place.
> —LIFE, April 17, 1944

GEORGE STROCK

" Here lie three Americans.

What shall we say of them? Shall we say that this is a noble sight? Shall we say that this is a fine thing, that they should give their lives for their country?

Or shall we say that this is too horrible to look at?

Why print this picture, anyway, of three American boys dead upon an alien shore? Is it to hurt people? To be morbid?

Those are not the reasons.

The reason is that words are never enough. The eye sees. The mind knows. The heart feels. But the words do not exist to make us see, or know, or feel what it is like, what actually happens. The words are never right.

Last winter, in the issue of February 22, we told about Bill, the Wisconsin boy; how he struggled through the dark and nervous jungle of New Guinea, stalking Japs like a cat; how he came at last to the blue sea at the rim of the jungle, and ran out onto the white beach, blazing mad; how the Japs got him there, suddenly, when the job was almost finished, so that he fell down on the sand, with his legs drawn up; and how the tide came in.

And we said then that we thought we ought to be permitted to show a picture of Bill—not just the words, but the real thing. We said that if Bill had the guts to take it, then we ought to have the guts to look at it.

Well, this is the picture.

And the reason we print it now is that, last week, President Roosevelt and Elmer Davis and the War Department decided that the American people ought to be able to see their own boys as they fall in battle; to come directly and without words into the presence of their own dead. "

—LIFE, September 20, 1943

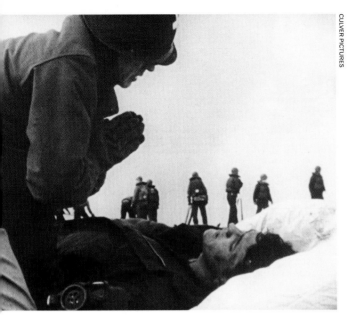

CULVER PICTURES

> The front was quiet in the early afternoon, except for artillery . . . There were many dead and many wounded, but the survivors contained the fluid situation and slowly turned it into a retreat, and finally, as the communiqué said, the bulge was ironed out. This was not done fast or easily; and it was not done by those anonymous things, armies, divisions, regiments. It was done by men, one by one—your men.
>
> —Martha Gellhorn, *The Face of War*

A Navy chaplain administers last rites aboard the USS *Franklin* (above); German prisoners (right) carry an American soldier killed during the Battle of the Bulge.

GEORGE SILK

Joseph, Francis, Albert, Madison and George Sullivan of Waterloo, Iowa, pleaded (bottom left) to serve in the Navy together. All five were killed when their ship was sunk by a Japanese submarine on November 13, 1942. The President sent condolences (below, a draft of his letter).

Dear Sir:
I have four brothers and two buddies from my Motorcycle club. I talked them into going into the U.S. Navy for the U.S.A. As a bunch, there is nobody that can beat us . . . I had four years training in the Navy and four in the National Guards. My brother had four years in the Navy and a couple years military training. Otherwise, any one of our brothers, which there are five of us and our two buddies, would like to stick together. We would all do our best to be as good as any other sailors in the Navy. We would appreciate it very much if you could, if possible, keep us together . . . I know I can make a first class team out of them.

—G.T. Sullivan, formerly USS *Hovey*

February 1, 1943

Dear Mr. and Mrs. Sullivan:

The knowledge that your five gallant sons are missing in action against the enemy inspires me to write you this personal message. I realize full well there is little I can say to assuage your grief.

As Commander-in-Chief of the Army and Navy, I want you to know that the entire nation shares in your sorrow. I offer you the gratitude of our country. We who remain to carry on the fight will maintain a courageous spirit, in the knowledge that such sacrifice is not in vain.

The Navy Department has informed me of the expressed desire of your sons, George Thomas, Francis Henry, Joseph Eugene, Madison Abel, and Albert Leo, to serve in the same ship. I am sure that we all take heart in the knowledge that they fought side by side. As one of your sons wrote, "We will make a team together that can't be beat." It is this spirit which in the end must triumph.

I send you my deepest sympathy in your hour of trial and pray that in Almighty God you will find the comfort and help that only He can bring.

Very sincerely yours,
FRANKLIN D. ROOSEVELT

Mr. and Mrs. T. F. Sullivan,
98 Adams Street,
Waterloo, Iowa.

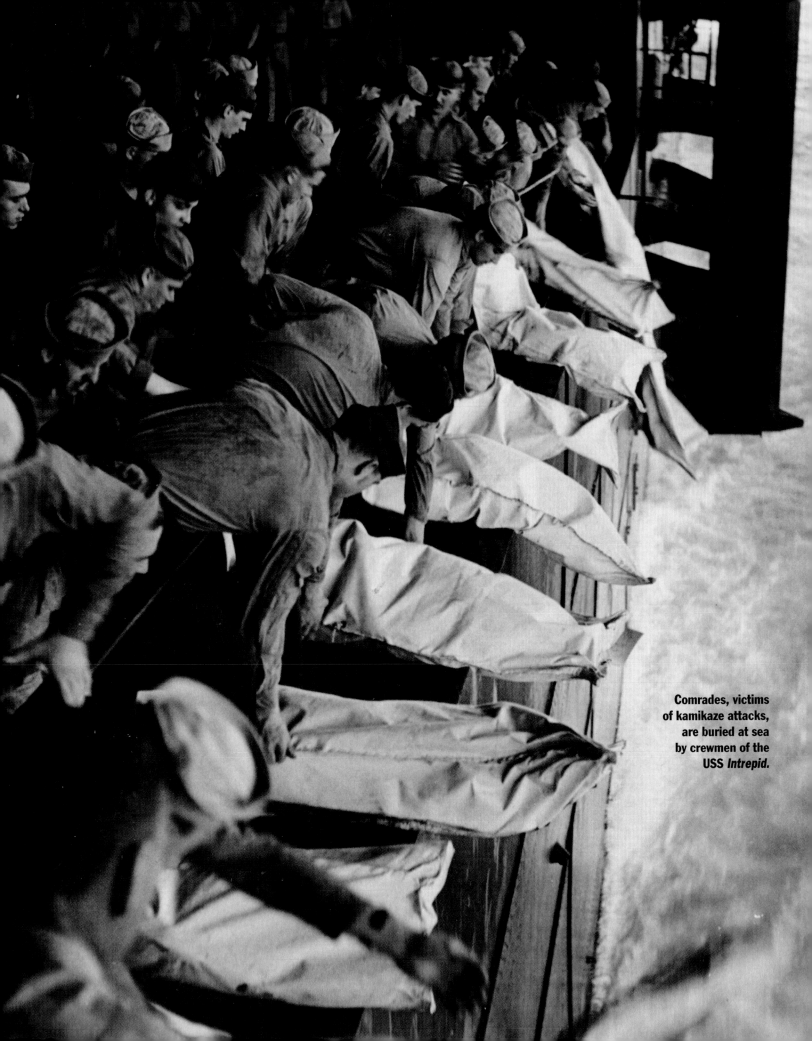

Comrades, victims
of kamikaze attacks,
are buried at sea
by crewmen of the
USS *Intrepid*.

> At the front lines in Italy: I was at the foot of the mule trail the night they brought Capt. [Henry T.] Waskow's body down . . . Two men unlashed his body from the mule and lifted it off and laid it in the shadow beside the low stone wall . . .
>
> The men in the road seemed reluctant to leave. They stood around, and gradually one by one I could sense them moving close . . .
>
> One soldier came and looked down, and he said out loud, 'God damn it.' That's all he said, and then he walked away . . .
>
> Another man came; I think he was an officer . . . [He] looked down into the dead captain's face, and then he spoke directly to him, as though he were alive. He said: 'I'm sorry, old man.'
>
> Then a soldier came and stood beside the officer, and bent over, and he too spoke to his dead captain, not in a whisper but awfully tenderly, and he said: 'I sure am sorry, sir.'
>
> Then the first man squatted down, and he reached down and took the dead hand, and he sat there for a full five minutes, holding the dead hand in his own and looking intently into the dead face, and he never uttered a sound all the time he sat there.
>
> And finally he put the hand down, and then reached up and gently straightened the points of the captain's shirt collar, and then he sort of rearranged the tattered edges of his uniform around the wound. And then he got up and walked away down the road in the moonlight, all alone.
>
> —Ernie Pyle, January 10, 1944

Colonel Francis I. Fenton kneels by the body of his son, also a member of the 1st Marine Division. Michael, a 19-year-old scout-sniper, was killed in action on Okinawa, May 7, 1945.

THE END

> **"** Sixteen hours ago an American airplane dropped one bomb on Hiroshima . . . If they do not now accept our terms, they may expect a rain of ruin from the air the likes of which has never been seen on this earth. **"**
>
> —President Truman
> August 6, 1945

> **"** Despite the best that has been done by everyone, the war situation has developed not necessarily to Japan's advantage. Moreover, the enemy has begun to employ a new and most cruel bomb. We have resolved to pave the way for a grand peace for all the generations to come by enduring the unendurable and suffering the insufferable. **"**
>
> —Emperor Hirohito
> August 14, 1945

News of the Japanese surrender has New Yorkers knee-deep in ticker tape on August 14, 1945.

AP

ANTHONY CALVACCA/NEW YORK POST

MYRON DAVIS

A Chicago mother (opposite) first sees headlines of the President's death and bursts into tears. Servicemen (above) read the news in New York.

"On Okinawa, with no time for grief, they went on with their work; but many a soldier wept . . . In an Omaha pool hall, men racked up their cues without finishing their games, walked out. In a Manhattan taxicab, a fare told the driver, who pulled over to the curb, sat with his head bowed . . .

It was the same in Washington, in the thousands on thousands of grief-wrung faces which walled the caisson's grim progression with prayers and with tears. It was the same on Sunday morning in the gentle landscape at Hyde Park, when the burial service of the Episcopal Church spoke its old, strong, quiet words of farewell; and it was the same at that later moment when all save the gravemen were withdrawn and reporters, in awe-felt hiding, saw how a brave woman, a widow, returned, and watched over the grave alone, until the grave was filled."

—James Agee, *Time*, April 23, 1945

After the two armies meet at the Elbe River in April, Russian and American soldiers take a comradely walk through Torgau, Germany.

" Men of the 69th Infantry Division sat on the banks of the Elbe in the warm sunshine today with no enemy in front or behind them and drank wine, cognac and vodka while they listened to their new Russian friends play accordions and sing Russian songs . . .

Russian soldiers are the most carefree bunch of screwballs that ever came together in an army. They would be best described as exactly like Americans—only twice as much. "

—Andy Rooney, *The Stars and Stripes,* April 28, 1945

U.S. SIGNAL CORPS

HULTON GETTY/LIAISON AGENCY

April 1945: In Eselheide,
Germany, jubilant Russians
hoist a Ninth Army soldier
who helped liberate
thousands of prisoners.

"For the first (and surely the only!) time in my life, I have been carried on shoulders like a football hero. And I've been bounced. ('Bouncing' appears to be a boisterous Slavic way of expressing enthusiastic liking—a couple of strapping fellows seize the object of their affections and toss him high in the air, catching him as he comes down and heaving him upward in flight once more. As they tire, two more huskies take over the game and continue from there.) They 'bounced' me in the building until my head ached from hitting the ceiling and I was powdered with fallen plaster dust. Then they carried me to the courtyard and bounced me some more. My pack fell off, I lost my helmet, I dropped my carbine . . . In a lull between bounces I grabbed desperately for my cigarettes and hastily began passing them out. That small gesture nearly finished me: I went down for the count under a fresh wave of kisses and impassioned bear hugs."

—Raymond Gantter, *Roll Me Over*

> **There were two rows of bodies stacked up like cordwood. They were thin and very white. Some of the bodies were terribly bruised, though there seemed to be little flesh to bruise. Some had been shot through the head, but they bled but little. All except two were naked. I tried to count them as best I could and arrived at the conclusion that all that was mortal of more than 500 men and boys lay there in two neat piles . . .**
>
> **I pray you to believe what I have said about Buchenwald. I have reported what I saw and heard, but only part of it. For most of it I have no words.**
>
> —Edward R. Murrow, radio broadcast, April 15, 1945

American soldiers and medics, stunned by the horrors of the concentration camps, are anxious to extend any possible aid to survivors, as here at Nordhausen.

In Blankenheim, a civilian rushes to surrender and to inform the Americans of the route taken by fleeing German SS troops.

U.S. ARMY PHOTOGRAPH

" First and Third Armies were advancing in mostly rural areas, untouched by the war. The GIs were spending their nights in houses. They would give the inhabitants five minutes or so to clear out. The German families were indignant. The GIs were insistent. As Lt. Max Lale put it in a March 30 letter home, 'None of us have any sympathy for them, because we all have been taught to accept the consequences of our actions—these people apparently feel they are the victims of something they had no hand in planning, and they seem to feel they are being mistreated.' "

—Stephen E. Ambrose
Citizen Soldiers

HULTON GETTY/LIAISON (2)

" During the liberation of Paris:
A thin, fair little woman and her husband came over to me. The woman said she was American, born in Syracuse. Her husband was French and she had been in Paris throughout the occupation. Her eyes were shining and she and her husband kept smiling widely, no matter what the conversation was about. 'You're the first American soldier I've seen,' she said, and started to lean over to kiss my cheek. Then she checked herself and turned to her husband. 'May I kiss him?' she asked, a little doubtfully. 'Certainly,' the husband said gravely. She kissed me on both cheeks. **"**

—Irwin Shaw, *The New Yorker,* August 25, 1945

**A Frenchwoman (left) extends
a now familiar greeting to
an American soldier. U.S.
servicemen (above) offer their
last predeparture sticks of gum
to British children.**

"Vive l'Amérique" rings out in Avranches, where a mademoiselle (left) expresses her gratitude to U.S. troops. Near Rome, a young boy (right) bestows flowers upon a weary American soldier.

> So many people swarmed around the Allied vehicles that a French soldier compared his tank to 'a magnet passing through a pile of steel filings.' A British journalist reported that 'the pent-up delirious crowds just wanted to touch us, to feel if we were real.' Soldiers were kissed until their faces turned red and hugged until they thought their ribs would crack. Girls clambered over tanks and trucks . . . Smiling civilians thrust long-hoarded bottles of fine wine, flowers and fruit at the soldiers—anything that might convey the gratitude they felt. One U.S. major counted a total of 67 bottles of champagne in his jeep by the time he reached the Seine.
>
> —*World War II: Liberation*

U.S. military personnel (left) unload some of the treasures recovered from Göring's cave near Königssee. A GI (above) examines a 15th century Eve while a second admires three paintings by Rembrandt and three by Cranach, also found among the looted art.

" The world's most incredible and most valuable private collection of art works was on view last week. The treasure (estimated value $200,000,000), private property of Hermann Göring, was discovered in the sealed room of an underground cave by troops of the U.S. 101st Airborne Division. All the facts on how Göring 'bought' these treasures are not known, but juggling of state funds and intimidation proved helpful. When the Wehrmacht began taking over one country after another, his collection began to grow and improve. He suddenly acquired Rubenses, Rembrandts, Van Dycks, Velázquezes, Botticellis. But not all of Göring's trophies were stolen: In the exhibit was an engraved silver cup which had been officially presented to Hermann Göring by the Hunting Master of the Reich, who was Hermann Göring. "

—LIFE, June 11, 1945

Aboard the aircraft carrier USS *Hoggatt Bay*, crewmembers celebrate with a spontaneous conga line after learning of Japan's surrender.

BROWN BROTHERS

" When the atom bombs were dropped and news began to circulate that 'Operation Olympic' would not, after all, be necessary, when we learned to our astonishment that we would not be obliged . . . to rush up the beaches near Tokyo assault-firing while being machine-gunned, mortared and shelled, for all the practiced phlegm of our tough facades we broke down and cried with relief and joy. We were going to live. We were going to grow to adulthood after all. The killing was all going to be over. "

—Paul Fussell, *Thank God for the Atom Bomb*

Two million people bent on celebrating news of the Japanese surrender still throng Times Square as night falls on August 14, 1945.

86th DIVISION
Blackhawks

COMING HOME

"The Jerries were shelling us again, fumbling for our positions . . . We watched the shells landing in the field around us . . . and in feeble bravado making small bets on the next hit.

I spent most of the long hours making plans for my homecoming. Each small detail was carefully polished to the last shining perfection. I debated seriously on small things. Which would be the perfect hour to come home? Early morning, late night, during a meal? Would I like the kids up and awake when I came in the door, or would the final drop of sweetness lie in arriving after dark, going up the stairs to the nursery, and opening the door softly . . . to see them warm in sleep, tousled and sweet-smelling?

It was an endless and intoxicating game."

—Raymond Gantter, *Roll Me Over*

Wildly cheering GIs in New York Harbor are members of the first combat division, the Blackhawks (86th Division of the U.S. Army), to return as a complete unit.

Many wounded men, like the soldiers on a Swedish ship arriving in New York (above), will be offered rehabilitation (right, a hospital in Hines, Ill.).

“ The wounded are coming home, and you will require an elementary manual of behavior toward these hurt men. It is essential that you realize that the men who are discharged from the armed forces are not cripples. They are men.

Be casual; be natural and considerate in your conversation. Treat the man as if he were the normal human being he was before he went away, for that is what he wants to be now. It may be necessary to be tough— not with him but with yourself. One of the most important things is not to show grief or pity. Exaggerated sympathy is far worse than no sympathy at all. ”

—LIFE, May 15, 1944

THOMAS D. MCAVOY

A father (left) who spent nearly four years in a Japanese prison camp is greeted by his son. A private first class and his dog (right) prepare to say their farewells on a dock in Karachi, India. Rules were stretched, however, and they were able to return to the U.S. together.

CULVER PICTURES

> 66 The telephone booths were mobbed by noisy, excited men. Now and then a man pushed out with tears on his cheeks: 'It was my mother. When she cried I couldn't hold it.' Nobody laughed or said a word. A ruddy-faced fighting man had said it for all as the train was rattling across the Jersey meadows that morning. He pressed close to the window and his eyes followed one spot on the moving, snow-covered landscape.
> 'That's my home,' he said. 'That's where I live.' 99
> —*Time*, January 22, 1945

Bridget Waters (above, at the U.S. embassy in England) is one of more than 100,000 overseas girls to marry U.S. servicemen. A shipload of GI brides (left) sets sail from Southampton, England, to join their American husbands.

> **"** Everything seemed shiny and new, the buildings reaching into the sky, the shiny cars and yellow cabs . . .
>
> Our destination was Grand Central Station, simply unbelievable to me after London's smoky late 19th century terminals. We paused at a snack bar. I was longing for a cup of tea. What I got was a tea bag in a cup of hot water. Was this how Americans drank tea? I also eyed the luscious cakes and pies, missing from England's bakeries even then . . . The man behind the counter said, 'No charge for the lady. After all those people went through in London, and still are rationed, it's my pleasure to do this.' **"**

—E.B. Shukert and B.S. Scibetta
War Brides of World War II

A returning serviceman lucky enough to catch a rare plane
ride home jumps right into the arms of his waiting family.

> " I lie around all day just dreaming of that wonderful moment when we see each other again. I know I'll really be excited. I want you to be waiting for me at the pier so I can run down the gangplank and into your arms. Gosh! What a wonderful thought. We would then grab a taxi and head for your hotel, providing of course I had a 24-hour pass. We could start catching up on some of our lovin' from there on out. It will take about 65 years for us to catch up on what we are missing now, and then I doubt if we ever can. Then home we go to see our little one. I can hardly wait to see him. This is my favorite daydream. "
>
> —Letter from 1st Lt. Charles O. Hardman to his wife, Mary, September 26, 1944

Sergeant Howard Kiyama, upon his homecoming to Honolulu, is welcomed by his father.

The great migration of homeward-bound soldiers continues. Most are as jubilant as this airman at Connecticut's Bradley Field, but not all are as expressive.

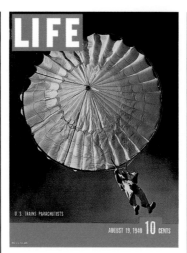

1939

August Germany and U.S.S.R. sign nonaggression pact.

September Germany invades Poland. Britain and France declare war; the U.S. remains neutral.

Germany and the Soviet Union divide Poland between them.

1940

February A barracks at Auschwitz, in Poland, is marked for conversion to a Nazi prison camp.

April Germany invades Norway and Denmark.

May Winston Churchill becomes British prime minister.

German forces invade France via the Netherlands, Belgium and Luxembourg.

Some 225,000 British troops, dispatched to France the previous autumn, and 140,000 other Allied troops begin a retreat from Dunkirk across the English Channel.

June Italy declares war on Britain and France.

France surrenders to Germany.

September The London Blitz begins; air raids will continue intermittently until May 1941.

Italian troops invade Egypt.

October Seventeen million American men register for the first peacetime draft in U.S. history.

German troops enter oil-rich Romania; Italy invades Greece.

November FDR wins an unprecedented third term.

Nazis round up Warsaw's Jews; some 450,000 are sealed in the ghetto.

1941

March FDR signs the Lend-Lease Act, allowing the U.S. to ship arms to Allied nations.

German Gen. Erwin Rommel begins an offensive in North Africa.

April Yugoslavia and Greece fall to Axis powers.

June Germany invades the Soviet Union, which will join the Allies.

August England and the Soviet Union conquer Iran.

September Germany lays siege to Leningrad and occupies Kiev.

The Nazi SS slaughters 33,771 Jews at Babi Yar in the Ukraine in two days.

November On the 24th, Roosevelt warns his Cabinet: "We are likely to be attacked within a week."

Despite intense winter weather, German forces advance to within a few miles of Moscow.

December The Japanese bomb Pearl Harbor; the U.S. declares war on Japan. Germany and Italy declare war on the U.S.

Japanese troops pour into neighboring southern Pacific and southeast Asian countries.

1942

January Gen. Douglas MacArthur completes his retreat from Manila

to the Bataan Peninsula.

At the Wannsee Conference in Berlin, Nazi officials approve the systematic extermination of European Jews.

February A week after Japanese forces land on Singapore Island, British troops surrender.

FDR authorizes the internment of at least 120,000 Japanese Americans.

March Japan defeats the Allies in the Battle of the Java Sea.

Proclaiming "I shall return," General MacArthur abandons the Philippines.

April Thousands of brutally abused Allied prisoners die on a forced trek to a prison camp—the Bataan Death March.

Lt. Col. James Doolittle's bombers attack Tokyo.

May The U.S. stops Japan in the Battle of the Coral Sea.

FDR creates the Women's Auxiliary Army Corps.

Some 11,500 Allied troops surrender on Corregidor Island.

June In the Battle of Midway—the turning point in the Pacific war— the U.S. Navy sinks four Japanese aircraft carriers.

The U.S. collects 30 million pounds of scrap rubber during a two-week drive.

Japan completes its conquest of the Philippines.

August American troops land on Guadalcanal.

German forces, 330,000 strong, attack Stalingrad.

October British rout Rommel's army from its positions in Egypt.

November Sixty-five thousand Allied troops led by General Eisenhower invade Algeria and Morocco.

Congress lowers the age of mandatory Selective Service registration to 18.

Soviets trap more than 250,000 German troops outside Stalingrad.

1943

January The Japanese begin to evacuate Guadalcanal.

February The last Germans at Stalingrad surrender, against Hitler's orders. About 500,000 Axis troops have died.

The U.S. approves rationing of such items as shoes, canned goods, meats and cheeses.

March German U-boat activity in the Atlantic reaches its peak.

May Allies successfully conclude the North African campaign.

The Germans quash the Warsaw ghetto uprising.

July Soviet troops win the war's largest tank battle, at Kursk, in the Ukraine.

The Allies invade Sicily.

September Italy surrenders; Allies land at Salerno to beat back Italy's German occupiers.

October The Allies move into Naples.

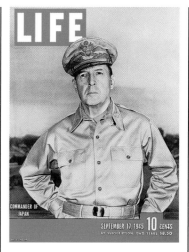

November Soviets retake Kiev.

The U.S. takes Makin quickly but faces greater Japanese resistance on Tarawa before securing the Gilbert Islands.

FDR, Churchill and Stalin have their first face-to-face meeting, in Tehran, to plan the invasion of France and discuss postwar Germany and Poland.

1944

January The Germans retreat from Leningrad, ending a 900-day siege during which a million residents of the city died from disease or starvation. Total Soviet deaths, military and civilian, will reach 27 million.

Allies land at Anzio to clear the way to Rome, but face counterattack along German defensive lines in Italy.

February During "Big Week," U.S. planes target German aircraft factories.

March The U.S. starts bombing Berlin.

U.S. forces encircle a Japanese holdout in Rabaul on New Britain Island, eventually isolating 100,000 enemy troops.

April A major U.S. attack surprises the Japanese on New Guinea.

May Allied troops break through German defenses in Italy.

June Allied forces enter Rome and chase the Germans north.

The largest amphibious invasion in history, Operation Overlord,

begins shortly before dawn on June 6. Nearly 130,000 Allied troops attack five beaches in Normandy, France.

The Japanese lose three aircraft carriers in the Battle of the Philippine Sea, the largest carrier battle of the war.

FDR signs the GI Bill, which offers financial and educational benefits to returning veterans.

July A bomb rips through Hitler's headquarters in East Prussia, though he avoids serious injury. The would-be assassins, Nazi officers, are executed.

Japan's prime minister, General Tojo, and his cabinet resign after a string of Pacific defeats.

August The U.S. captures Guam.

The Allies secure southern France.

Soviet troops reach the German border.

French-led forces expel the Germans from Paris.

September U.S. Army troops breach the German border for the first time.

October Athens is liberated.

Reprisals for an uprising against German occupiers leave 200,000 Poles dead; Warsaw is destroyed.

The Allies capture their first German city, Aachen.

MacArthur returns to the Philippines; the U.S. defeats Japanese naval forces in the Battle of Leyte Gulf.

In Moscow, Churchill and Stalin agree on a division of Eastern Europe into spheres of influence.

November FDR soundly defeats Thomas Dewey to win his fourth term as President.

1945

January Auschwitz, the largest Nazi extermination camp, is liberated. Six million Jews and millions of others died during the Holocaust.

The Allies win the Battle of the Bulge, also known as the Battle of the Ardennes, in Belgium and Luxembourg.

Soviet troops secure Warsaw and move to within 50 miles of Berlin.

February In Yalta, the Big Three fix postwar borders for Germany and Poland and discuss the formation of the United Nations.

Six U.S. Marines raise the American flag over Iwo Jima; in weeks, the island is secure.

Allied bombing of Dresden kills 60,000 people; most are civilians.

March U.S. bombing of Tokyo kills more than 80,000.

April Soviets capture Vienna and begin the final assault on Berlin.

FDR dies; Vice President Harry S Truman is sworn in as President.

U.S. and Soviet troops meet for the first time, in Torgau, Germany.

Italian partisans execute Mussolini and his mistress.

Hitler and his lover, Eva Braun, marry and later commit suicide.

May Berlin falls to Soviet forces.

Germany surrenders May 7 at Eisenhower's headquarters in Reims and a day later to the Soviets in Berlin. May 8 is celebrated as V-E (Victory in Europe) Day.

June The four occupying powers formally assume command of Germany.

Fifty countries sign the U.N. charter in San Francisco.

July The U.S. Army captures Okinawa after a three-month fight.

U.S. victory in the Philippines ends an eight-month campaign.

The first atomic bomb is detonated, in New Mexico.

Clement Attlee replaces Churchill as prime minister.

August The U.S. drops atomic bomb on Hiroshima and, three days later, Nagasaki.

U.S.S.R. declares war on Japan.

Japan agrees to unconditional surrender.

The Allies divide Korea, previously controlled by Japan, along the 38th parallel. The Soviets occupy the north, Americans the south.

September The Japanese formally surrender aboard the USS *Missouri* in Tokyo Bay. Americans observe V-J (Victory over Japan) Day.

American battle-related deaths total 291,557. Estimated military and civilian deaths the world over reach 55 million.

Picture and text sources

are listed by page.

7-8, 11: Copied by Henry Groskinsky. 24: "Rosie the Riveter," lyric © 1942, renewed by Music Sales Corp. (ASCAP) and Fred Ahlert Music Corp.; international copyright secured; all rights reserved; reprinted by permission of Music Sales Corp. and Fred Ahlert Music Corp. 44: Brendan Gill, "X, B, and Chiefly A," originally published in *The New Yorker,* June 13, 1942; reprinted by permission of the Gill family. 51: Ted Nakashima, "Concentration Camp: U.S. Style," originally published in *The New Republic,* June 15, 1942. 52: "As Time Goes By," lyric © 1931 (renewed) Warner Bros. Inc., all rights reserved, used by permission, Warner Bros. Publications U.S. Inc., Miami, FL 33014. 54: Photo and letter courtesy of the Marshall C. Nichols family; copied by Steven Freeman. 55: Photo and letter courtesy of the Simpson family; copied by Steven Freeman. 57: Letter courtesy of Mrs. Jean Fisher Hall. 76: A.J. Liebling, "Quest for Mollie," originally published in *The New Yorker,* May 26 and June 2, 1945; © 1945 A.J. Liebling, renewed 1977 Norma Liebling Stonehill; reprinted by permission of Russell & Volkening as agents for the author. 112: "I Left My Heart at the Stage Door Canteen," lyric © 1942 Irving Berlin, © renewed Irving Berlin, © assigned to Winthrop Rutherfurd Jr., Anne Phipps Sidamon-Eristoff and Theodore R. Jackson as Trustees of the God Bless America Fund; international copyright secured; all rights reserved; reprinted by permission. 125: John Steinbeck, "Once There Was a War," © 1943, 1958 John Steinbeck; renewed 1971 Elaine Steinbeck, John Steinbeck IV and Thomas Steinbeck; used by permission of Viking Penguin, a division of Penguin Putnam Inc. 131: Ernie Pyle, "Wounded and Trapped," reprinted by permission of Scripps Howard Foundation. 136: Photo and artifacts courtesy of the Jack Wilkes family. 152: Copied by Henry Groskinsky. 154: Ernie Pyle, "The Death of Captain Waskow," reprinted by permission of Scripps Howard Foundation. 186: Letter courtesy of the Charles O. Hardman family.

To share your resources with others

More than a half century has passed since the end of World War II, and many of those who could speak or write of it have been lost to us forever. For every story not told, the world is poorer—but it is not too late to add to our store of information.

If you would like to contribute to our knowledge of the war, there are collections and organizations that can help. Among them:

The Institute on World War II and the Human Experience, in the history department at Florida State University, aims to collect and preserve letters, diaries, official histories, photos, newsletters, personnel documents and personal accounts of World War II—anything and everything that is on paper. The Institute's Web address is www.fsu.edu/~ww2

The Legacy Project is a national, all-volunteer organization that works to remember and honor men and women who have served this nation in wartime by seeking out and preserving their letters. Photocopies of letters can be sent to:
The Legacy Project
Attn: Andrew Carroll
P.O. Box 53250
Washington, DC 20009

The Women in Military Service for America Memorial accepts photographs, objects, letters and other documents related to women's military service.
www. womensmemorial.org

The National D-Day Museum, in New Orleans, accepts objects, letters and other documents relevant both to World War II campaigns and to the home front.
E-mail:
curator@ddaymuseum.org

A debt of gratitude is owed to the people who worked on this book:

Associate Picture Editors Suzanne Hodgart, Christina Lieberman

Picture Researcher Joan Shweky

Research Chief Deirdre Van Dyk

Researchers Hildegard Anderson, Lela Nargi, Eric Roston, Ben Nugent (assistant)

Art Assistant Lauren Steel

Copy Chief Kathleen Berger, and all members of the LIFE Copy Department

Special thanks to Dr. William Donnelly, U.S. Army Center of Military History.